881400

DATE DUE

DE 16 '9	OC 2 1 '96	NO 9 '99	
SE 20 '9	NO 2 6 '96		
AP 1 0 '96	DE 13 '96		
MY 4 '9	MY 13 '97		
JY 1 0 '96	DE 02 '97		
JY 2 3 '96	DE 1 1 '97		
SE 1 8 '96	AP 2 '98		
OC 3 '96	OC 07 '98		
	NO 23 '98		

AP 30 34
MY 26 '9
JY 18 '9
OC 6 '9

NO 28 '9

The
Abortion
Controversy

THE

Abortion Controversy

CAROL A. EMMENS

JULIAN MESSNER ⓂⓂ NEW YORK
A Division of Simon & Schuster, Inc.

Published by Julian Messner,
A Division of Simon & Schuster, Inc.
Simon & Schuster Building
Rockefeller Center
1230 Avenue of the Americas
New York, New York 10020

JULIAN MESSNER and colophon are
trademarks of Simon & Schuster, Inc.

Manufactured in the United States of America

Design by Claire Counihan

10 9 8 7 6 5 4 3 2 1
10 9 8 7 6 5 4 3 2 1 (pbk)

Library of Congress Cataloging-in-Publication Data

Emmens, Carol A.
   The abortion controversy.

   Bibliography: p.
   Includes index.

   Summary: Examines the controversial issue of abortion,
including its moral, legal, social, and medical aspects.
   1. Abortion—United States—Juvenile literature.
2. Abortion—Law and legislation—United States—
Juvenile literature. [1. Abortion] I. Title.
HQ767.5.U5E45   1987   363.4'6'0973   86-28532

ISBN 0-671-62284-6

ISBN 0-671-64209-X pbk

Contents

ONE   Introduction to the Controversy   *1*

TWO   Abortion and the Individual   *7*

THREE   The Sides –   *24*

FOUR   The Supreme Court Decision –   *40*

FIVE   Leading up to Roe   *47*

SIX   Attempts to Overturn Roe   *58*

SEVEN   Further Appeals to the Supreme Court   *75*

EIGHT   The Right-to-Life Movement and Protest –   *84*

NINE   Abortion in the Past   *96*

TEN   Abortion Around the World –   *108*

ELEVEN   Conclusion   *125*

Selected Bibliography   *129*

Index   *133*

ONE

Introduction to the Controversy

The issue of abortion has been extremely controversial. On January 22, 1973, the Supreme Court of the United States handed down two rulings that made abortion legal nationally. The rulings were based on the cases *Roe* v. *Wade,* to which people generally refer, and *Doe* v. *Bolton.* The Court's decisions did not end the debate over abortion. Instead, it was like adding fuel to a fire. The two sides in the debate—the prochoice groups, or advocates of legal abortion, and the anti-abortion, or right-to-life, groups—lined up to fight for their own beliefs. The anti-abortion movement went into full swing, and the prochoice groups countered with their own campaigns.

Everyone agrees that taking a life, except in self-defense, is morally wrong. The Fourteenth Amendment of our Constitution guarantees that "no person shall

. . . be deprived of life, liberty or property without due process of law." That makes the controversy over abortion based on the question, "When does the fetus become a person?"

There is no single, definitive answer to that question, although historically and legally the fetus has not been regarded as a person. Even medicine does not provide a clear-cut answer. In testimony before the Senate, Dr. Lewis Thomas of the Memorial Sloan-Kettering Cancer Center in New York said that "the question of when human life begins . . . lies beyond the reach of science." Over 1,300 scientists from universities across the country signed a petition agreeing with him.

People base their beliefs as to when a fetus becomes a "person" on their background, religion, experience, and philosophy. Nevertheless, people who practice the same religion or hold the same jobs do not necessarily agree with one another.

There are various stages in the development of the fetus from a single cell to a baby. Scientists do agree on the facts about the development of the fetus, but they disagree on the interpretation of the facts.

There are many views on when a fetus becomes a person. That means there are many views about when an abortion is acceptable and when it is not.

Some people feel that human life begins when the mother's egg is united with the father's sperm. The moment when the egg and the sperm unite is known as conception. The fertilized egg is a living human substance. But is the fertilized egg, known at this stage as a zygote, a human being? There are those who answer "Yes." They point to the fact that the zygote contains

DNA (deoxyribonucleic acid), which transmits hereditary characteristics.

Many people view the fertilized egg as a potential
human life. The fertilized egg is not a complete human
being; it is not simply a small body that has to grow
larger. It needs to develop from a single cell to a
complete individual, just as an acorn has to develop into
an oak tree. The human individual develops biologically
in a continuous fashion. We could therefore consider
the possibility that the rights of a human person might
develop in the same way.

Once the egg is fertilized, it has to travel up the
fallopian tubes to the uterus. Only one-third to one-half
of the fertilized eggs successfully reach the uterus; it
takes about five days. It takes about four more days for it
to implant itself in the uterus. There are birth control
devices, such as intrauterine devices (IUDs), which are
thought to prevent implantation. To some, the implantation of the zygote is the start of human life.

At the end of fourteen days, the zygote is known as
an embryo. Between the seventh and fourteenth days,
an egg sometimes divides itself—in one out of ninety
pregnancies—and twins develop. There are those who
argue that a human being cannot divide into two;
therefore, the embryo is not a human being until after
the "twinning stage."

The embryo undergoes several stages of development
between the fourth and eighth week, when it becomes
known as the fetus. The stages vary from fetus to fetus,
but generally around the fourth week, the heart begins
to beat. Around the sixth week, the nervous system
begins to develop. Sometime between the sixth and

eighth week, all the organs develop in a primitive way. There are people who point to each of these stages as the beginning of life.

There are those who feel the fetus is not a human being until it is viable, or can live outside the womb. Generally, the fetus is not viable until sometime between the twenty-fourth and twenty-eighth weeks. Adding to the controversy over abortion, however, are the continuing medical advances that enable doctors to keep a fetus alive—generally for only hours or days—at earlier and earlier stages of development. Doctors set their own limits on the latest stage in pregnancy when they will perform an abortion, because they are afraid to abort a viable fetus. Different states also have laws limiting when a woman can have a legal abortion.

There are people who believe that the fetus becomes a "person" when its brain develops. The development of the cerebral part of the brain begins around the twenty-eighth week. By the end of the thirty-second week, it is well developed. In both the medical and legal professions, "brain death," or the lack of brain waves, is recognized as the end of life. Since the death of the brain is considered the end of life, many people feel that the beginning of brain life should be considered the beginning of human life. Often, people who are labeled "brain dead" are taken off machines, such as respirators, that artificially keep their bodies functioning. Before life-support systems were invented, the brain died minutes after the lungs and heart stopped working. Now machines can keep the lungs and heart functioning despite massive brain damage and an apparently irreversible coma. But does a human being still exist? Most people today feel the answer is no. Defining "death" is important because of the growing number of organ transplants. In such cases, the organs have to be removed without delay, but it is legally necessary to declare the person dead before removing an organ.

At the far end of the spectrum are those few who feel the fetus is not a human being until it is actually born. They approve of abortion at any stage of the pregnancy.

Because of the strong emotions the issue of abortion generates, the debate sometimes deteriorates into bitter name-calling confrontations. The anti-abortionists call themselves "prolife," which makes their anti-abortion position sound positive. They refer to the prochoice groups as pro-abortion, which makes them sound in favor of abortion. The prochoice groups contend that nobody "favors" abortion, but that every woman should be free to choose for herself.

Abortion is a moral, medical, legal, and social problem. It affects the very fabric of our society, including the laws, the structure of the family, and the role of women. It raises many questions for the women who are faced with an unwanted pregnancy, for their husbands and lovers, and for the community as a whole. It is a very private matter with serious public implications, and that's why it is a complex issue, difficult to address. For some people, abortion is a black-and-white issue —it's either right or it's wrong. Yet for the majority of people, it is a gray area. According to a 1985 *Newsweek* poll, about 45 percent of the people surveyed were not positive that their position on abortion was "right": less than 25 percent were certain they took the correct position.

Novelist Anna Quindlen supports legal abortion; however, she has some reservations. In an essay in the *New York Times,* she wrote that she used to think an abortion was a woman's absolute right. Now she wonders if an abortion is moral for the woman in a stable marriage. She admitted, "I don't feel all one way about abortion anymore, and I don't think it serves a just cause to pretend that many of us do."

Often, it seems as though people are torn between polar opposites when it comes to the issue of abortion. Actually, most people share Anna Quindlen's mixed feelings about abortion. They may support legal abortion but would not undergo an abortion themselves or they may only support abortion in certain cases. Whatever individuals feel, it is clear that abortion is an important and controversial issue.

T W O

Abortion and the Individual

There are two types of abortion—spontaneous and induced. A spontaneous abortion, generally called a miscarriage, occurs in approximately 15 percent of all pregnancies. Most spontaneous abortions occur in the first three months, or first trimester, of pregnancy and are usually attributed to an abnormality in the fetus. Miscarriages are more common for older women and women who had difficulty becoming pregnant.

An induced abortion occurs when the fetus is forced to leave the uterus and dies as a result. This is the type of abortion that is creating such controversy. There is divided opinion about whether an induced abortion increases the chances of spontaneous abortion in later pregnancies.

Pregnancy is a major event for any woman regardless of whether or not she welcomes it. It is a time of stress.

· 7 ·

It changes her relationships, her self-image, her body, and her goals. It is a time of worry, because pregnancy carries a small health risk. When the pregnancy is unwanted, the experience is doubly stressful. Now the woman is faced with a very difficult decision—should she have the child or should she have an abortion?

Approximately 1.5 million women each year in the United States decide to have an abortion. Almost one-fourth of all pregnancies today are ended by induced abortions; that's four thousand a day. Abortion is the most frequently performed medical procedure in the United States. Since January 22, 1973, abortion has been legal nationally in the United States. As a result, individual states cannot completely ban abortion. In general, abortion is legal until the fetus is considered capable of living outside the womb.

Abortion Methods

When a woman misses her menstrual period and she does not want to be pregnant, she can undergo what is called "menstrual regulation" within two weeks of her missed period. Technically, menstrual regulation is not seen as an abortion, because it is performed before a woman's pregnancy is confirmed. The contents of the uterus are withdrawn by suction. Some women who are not pregnant need menstrual regulation to keep their cycle regular. As an abortion method menstrual regulation, which is also known as menstrual extraction, has a 5 percent failure rate.

Once the pregnancy is confirmed and the woman decides not to continue with it, there are several ways for a doctor to perform an abortion. The most common method is suction, which is used in the first trimester. Nearly 90 percent of all abortions are carried out during the first trimester. Usually, a local anesthetic is injected into the cervix, which as a result becomes numb. The local anesthetic allows the woman to be awake throughout the operation. The cervix is dilated, and a tube attached to a suction machine is inserted. The fetal tissue is sucked up through the tube. Then an instrument called a curette is used to get rid of any clots of tissue that are left. A suction abortion takes only five to ten minutes. It is generally done in a clinic or outpatient ward. Immediately afterward, the woman may feel dizzy or nauseated for a brief time. Normally, the woman experiences cramps similar to those of a menstrual period, but they do not last longer than a few hours.

A second method usually used between the twelfth and fourteenth weeks is called "dilation and curettage" (D & C). The woman is put to sleep with a general anesthetic. The cervix is dilated, and the doctor removes the fetus, using a scraping instrument.

A third method, also used after the twelfth week, is known as "dilation and evacuation" (D & E). After the woman is put to sleep, the doctor widens the opening of the uterus with dilators, crushes the fetus, and then extracts it with forceps. Many doctors refuse to perform D & E operations because crushing the fetus puts a psychological strain on them and the staff.

The saline abortion method is used during the period, lasting from the thirteenth week to the twenty-sixth week, known as the second trimester, although abortions are not performed after twenty-four weeks. It is a method that is similar to childbirth and requires hospitalization. A saline, or salt, solution is inserted into the uterus, causing the woman to go into labor. The fetus is almost always killed by the saline solution before the woman goes into labor. It takes an average of nineteen hours and is unpleasant for the woman, doctor, and staff. There is a slight danger that the saline solution will seep into the woman's bloodstream and cause hemorrhages, or lung and kidney damage.

A technique similar to the saline solution method utilizes prostaglandin injections, which cause the woman to go into labor. The prostaglandins almost always cut off the supply of oxygen to the fetus, which causes it to die. There have been very rare instances, however, of the live birth of a fetus after prostaglandin injections. Many doctors do not perform abortions after the twentieth week because they do not want to risk killing a fetus that could be capable of living on its own. Some doctors set their own personal limits at even earlier stages. Still others do not perform D & Es or saline abortions at all. This may not be a moral decision —rather a matter of personal choice.

Only 0.9 percent of all abortions are performed after twenty weeks. Generally, when women have late abortions it's because they have not received the results of prenatal tests until then.

After twenty-four weeks, no abortions are performed. Occasionally, health problems, such as toxemia (poisoning of the blood), force the doctor to induce premature birth. In those instances, doctors try to save the life of both the infant and the mother.

Abortions are generally viewed as medically safe and simple. It is 352 times safer to have an abortion than to

have an appendix removed. But, like all medical procedures, abortions are not without risks. The complications are related to the abortion method, the age of the
woman, the number of childbirths or abortions she has
had, and the length of the pregnancy. The most common aftereffects are infections, cramps, lacerations,
bleeding, and injury to the cervix or uterus. Antibiotics
are sometimes prescribed to avoid the risk of infection.
In addition, the woman is told not to douche, use
tampons, or have intercourse for three weeks. In rare
cases, the woman can suffer from an allergic reaction to
the medication.

The risk of complications increases with the length of
the pregnancy. After the eighth week of pregnancy, the
risk of death for the woman is three times greater than
before; after the twentieth week, the risk is forty-five
times greater. Nevertheless, the risk of death still is very
small. A woman is eleven times more likely to die from
childbirth than from an abortion. In contrast, illegal
abortions were, and are, much more dangerous than
legal ones. Frequently, women were severely injured,
suffered hemorrhages, or went into shock.

Having an abortion sometimes causes a woman to
worry about her ability to become pregnant in the
future. It should not be difficult to become pregnant
again unless there were very severe complications from
the abortion. In fact, the menstrual cycle can begin
within a few days after the abortion. Sometimes women
think this bleeding is caused by the abortion. Many
doctors, therefore, prescribe birth control pills to be
taken immediately. This puts the woman's system back
into a predictable monthly cycle.

A legal abortion is physically a routine matter in nearly all cases. Even so, an abortion is rarely easy for a woman because of the emotional and psychological factors involved.

Who Has an Abortion?

Women from all walks of life, from all religious groups, from all races, and from all economic and social classes have abortions. There are particular patterns. For example, in the United States, the abortion rate for black women, who make up approximately 10 percent of the total women in the population, is double that for white women.

The majority of those who have abortions are in their twenties. The next highest group is single, teenage women. This group makes up nearly 40 percent. Some of the teenagers are so young that they do not even understand the connection between sexual intercourse and pregnancy.

Teens are sometimes reluctant to practice birth control because it is not "romantic." Because she may be in love, often for the first time, a teenage girl may believe her sexual partner when he says she will not become pregnant or that they will get married if she does.

As a group, teenagers are very lax about using birth control, or contraception. On the average, teenagers are sexually active for nine months before using birth control. Sometimes it is hard or embarrassing for them to obtain birth control pills or contraceptive devices. The most effective methods of birth control require a doctor's prescription—for example, the pill—or require insertion or fitting—an IUD or a diaphragm.

Because of this, teens sometimes use "homemade" birth control devices, such as condoms made from cellophane. They do not work. Those who do use birth control are often casual about it, using it in a haphazard way.

Teenagers are often ignorant about how birth control works. Many do not realize the danger of skipping their birth control pills for a day or two. Says one girl, "I never dreamed it was possible to get pregnant just because I missed a pill or two." In addition, many women, particularly teenagers, believe in myths regarding birth control. For example, they believe that douching with certain substances prevents pregnancy. It doesn't!

In addition, teenagers are at the most fertile period in their lives and no method of birth control is 100 percent effective. The pill is 99 percent effective, while condoms or diaphragms are 90–95 percent effective, and IUDs are about 97 percent effective.

Teenagers have a high rate—about 44 percent—of late abortions, which are performed about the twentieth week. This is because teens are more likely to ignore, deny, or misunderstand the signs that they are pregnant. When they do know that they are pregnant, they are often afraid to tell their parents or their friends, so they put it off until it is obvious. Many of them think their parents will throw them out of the house, or they fantasize that they want to have a baby to love. Others spend weeks debating whether to have an abortion or to get married and give birth.

Teenagers are also more likely to have repeat abortions. Repeat abortions often seem to be the result of poor self-esteem and the need to find love. Sometimes having sex makes teens feel they are grown up; sometimes it is seen as a way to save a threatened relationship. Getting pregnant can be a way for a girl to get her parents or her boyfriend to show concern for her.

Teenagers who have abortions do not necessarily approve of them, especially for married women. These young people will have an abortion because they simply cannot cope with and care for a baby.

Why Do Women Have Abortions?

There are many reasons why women choose to have an abortion instead of carrying the fetus to term. The most common reasons are that they are too young, they are single or in the midst of a divorce, they are pregnant as a result of rape or incest, they have as many children as they want, they are medically at risk, they cannot financially afford a child, or they know the fetus is abnormal.

The circumstances in which a woman seeks an abortion frequently color the way her friends and family view her action. Family members and friends often encourage the woman to have an abortion if she has health problems, has been raped, or is single. The same people may condemn her for having an abortion if she is happily married. Far fewer people approve of abortions for economic or personal reasons—if for example, a job promotion is at stake—than for reasons of health, rape, incest, or fetal abnormalities. Even so, all over the world, whether abortions are legal or illegal, the vast majority of them are performed for social or economic reasons. The most common of these reasons are poverty, poor housing, divorce, illegitimacy, drug addiction, and wanting to limit the number of children born.

Among the most difficult abortions for women to face are those that are done because the fetus suffers from genetic abnormalities. It is possible to detect some fetal abnormalities by the medical procedure known as amniocentesis. Amniocentesis is the withdrawal of amniotic fluid from the sac surrounding the fetus. After it is withdrawn, the fluid is analyzed.

A major disadvantage of amniocentesis is that it cannot be done until the woman is at least thirteen weeks pregnant, and the results of the tests are not known for two to six more weeks. Fortunately, in about 95 percent of the cases in which a woman has amniocentesis, the procedure shows that the fetus is not suffering from the abnormalities that would be detectable by this method. Estimates indicate that a very small proportion of abortions—between one in a thousand and thirty in a thousand—are performed because the fetus is abnormal. In these cases, the abortion is late and is more dangerous as well as more psychologically difficult.

A new procedure for testing the fetus is chorionic villus biopsy. A sample of tissue from the amniotic sac is taken out and analyzed. The chief advantage of this procedure is that it can be done at eight weeks and the results are back by the twelfth week. The major disadvantage is that it is riskier for the fetus and it is not yet used routinely.

Women over the age of 35 are recommended to have amniocentesis because they have a greater chance of giving birth to a retarded child than younger women. Doctors also recommend it when there is a family history of a detectable disease. Amniocentesis reveals that the fetus has genetic disorders, such as sickle-cell anemia; Down's syndrome, or mental retardation; and Tay-Sachs, a neurological disease that causes a painful death within a few years. Certain conditions are more prevalent among certain groups than others. For example, sickle-cell anemia is more prevalent among blacks than whites and Tay-Sachs is more prevalent among Jews than other groups. Unfortunately, for defects such as Down's syndrome, it is possible to learn whether or not the fetus has it, but it is impossible to know how severe it will be. The child may be severely retarded or only slightly retarded.

Sometimes there is the possibility of fetal abnormality but no way to test for it. For example, women who get rubella, or German measles, during the first three months of their pregnancy run the risk of having an abnormal child with defects. If the mother catches rubella after the first three months, the risk to the fetus is negligible because it is more fully developed. The most common fetal disabilities caused by German measles are cataracts, deafness, congenital heart disease, bone lesions, and physical and mental retardation.

If the fetus does have a disability caused by German measles, statistically it is more likely to be minor. It is then up to the woman to decide whether she wants to take even a very small risk of bearing a child with a disability. She is faced with serious questions: Is she able to take care of a child with a disability? How will it affect the family? Will it place a financial burden on the family? Will it place an emotional strain on her, her husband, or her other children? Will she love the child or will she be repelled? Those are questions that are close to impossible to answer before the birth. Some women decide not to "take a chance" on giving birth to a disabled child and have an abortion.

The surgeon general of the United States, C. Everett Coop, describes amniocentesis as a "search and destroy mission." Others feel it is immoral to bring a child into the world knowing it will face hardship or possibly a painful death within a few days or few years.

On the positive side, there are tests that make it easier for a woman to complete her pregnancy without worry. It is now possible to test the fetus to determine whether it has hemophilia, a hereditary disorder in which the blood does not clot. Hemophilia usually only shows in boys. About one in 6,500 have the disease. It is passed on to the child by the mother. In the past, if there was a history of hemophilia in the family, amniocentesis was performed to determine if the fetus was a boy. If so, it had an even chance of having the disorder. Some women chose to abort and only carry female fetuses to term. Now the new test can tell the woman in advance whether the male fetus is a hemophiliac. If not, she can complete her pregnancy without worry. If so, she has the option of having an abortion. It is not an easy decision to make, however, for hemophiliacs can, and do, lead happy lives. Who can say in advance whether or not a hemophiliac will lead a productive life or a miserable one?

Because of medical advances in prenatal testing, today's woman has to think about the quality of life and the length of life the fetus can be expected to have. These factors weigh heavily in the abortion dilemma.

For example, fetal testing can reveal the presence of Huntington's chorea, a rare hereditary disorder. In the past, this was not detectable until the first symptoms appeared, generally at the age of thirty or forty. Huntington's chorea begins with loss of coordination. As it progresses, the victim suffers from psychological problems and emotional outbursts, and finally dies. It is not easy for a woman to choose to give birth to a person who will live half of the usual life expectancy and who will suffer a horrible death. Yet abortion is not an easy choice either.

As science discovers new ways to test fetuses for disorders, women will be faced with even more difficult choices. It's expected that there will be a test for cystic fibrosis, an incurable hereditary disease that causes chronic lung problems. It generally kills by late childhood or early adulthood.

Whatever her motivation for getting one, an abortion is not what a woman wants, but what she feels is necessary given her circumstances.

The Psychological Effects

ᛗ An abortion can sometimes cause emotional or psychological problems. They are generally considered minor upsets, however. According to the Institute of Medicine of the National Academy of Sciences, there is no evidence of serious mental illness caused by having an abortion. ↙

Some women do experience feelings of guilt or depression after having an abortion. A woman may feel guilty for a wide variety of reasons: abortion may be against her religious beliefs; she failed to use birth control; or her only motivation for getting it done was that she didn't want children at that particular time. When a woman has an abortion in a hospital, she is usually placed on the same floor as the maternity ward. That can cause additional emotional stress.

Even women who used a birth control method that failed sometimes blame themselves for the pregnancy. Those who neglected to use birth control may feel even worse. In some instances, they intended to abstain from sex but didn't. Their intentions were probably unrealistic. However, sex itself still causes feelings of guilt because some people say it is "wrong" or "bad" unless the couple is married. As a result, some women do not admit even to themselves that they are going to have sex, so they end up without protection.

Some women who have abortions feel guilty because they—or their friends—label their action "selfish." They may want children, but not at that time in their lives. They may feel they are too young or too involved in their careers. They may want to finish school or to relocate. They may feel that they do not want to be tied down with a child.

When a woman has an abortion in opposition to her religious background, it can make her feel she is immoral. Even religious leaders have found themselves in a quandary when they or their wives or daughters are faced with an unexpected pregnancy. Said a minister, "I always told friends I'd never have an abortion, but I found I had no alternative."

Nurses working in clinics report that women have

come in for abortions wearing "Right to Life" buttons. A teenager with a strong religious background said that abortion is "murder, but it's justifiable homicide."

Women are sometimes well into their pregnancy when they find out that the fetus is abnormal. The choice between carrying the pregnancy, which may have been wanted, and aborting can be a wrenching emotional decision, especially if the pregnancy had been planned.

A young woman whose family had a history of serious medical problems underwent amniocentesis. She learned that the female fetus that she was carrying had several abnormalities, so she decided to have an abortion. She became pregnant again, this time with twins. Once again, she decided to undergo amniocentesis. But twins develop in separate sacs, and the doctor was successful in obtaining fluid from only one sac. There was no way to tell if the second twin had abnormalities. To the doctor's surprise, the woman was not upset, but relieved. Now she felt that regardless of what the prenatal tests showed about the one twin, she could continue her pregnancy for the sake of the other.

Obviously, a great number of factors are at work when a woman is faced with an unwanted pregnancy. Because of the stress, many clinics offer counseling services or request that the woman return after thinking about the abortion for a few days. Counselors sometimes advise against the abortion if they feel the woman really does not want it or cannot handle it. The vast majority of the clinics also provide birth control information as part of their service. In contrast to the women who feel guilty are those who do not and who then suffer guilt feelings for not feeling guilty.

It is worth noting that more women are depressed following childbirth than following an abortion. After childbirth, many women have the "baby blues," or postpartum depression. In part, this feeling is caused by hormonal changes in the body.

The Role of the Male, Family, and Friends

The relationship with the father of the child affects how the woman feels about the abortion. When the relationship is a good one, it probably poses more mixed feelings than when it is bad. Married women often feel more guilty about having an abortion than unmarried women. In an article in the *New York Times*, May 1976, a married woman wrote:

> And it certainly does make more sense not to be having a baby right now—we say that to each other all the time. But I have this ghost now. A very little ghost that only appears when I'm seeing something beautiful, like the full moon on the ocean last weekend. And the baby waves at me. And I wave at the baby. "Of course, we have room," I cry to the ghost. "Of course, we do."

The writer Linda Francke supports abortion, but she feels that having an abortion causes many women to have all types of emotions: indecision, regret, relief, guilt, loss of interest in sex. She feels that the emotional impact of an abortion has to be recognized and accepted.

Frequently, having an abortion changes the relationship between the man and woman involved. It can strengthen the relationship if it was good originally. On the other hand, it sometimes puts a barrier between the man and the woman and causes the relationship to end. The woman sometimes blames the man for either the pregnancy or the abortion and becomes bitter. Some women swear they will never have a second abortion.

An abortion can be especially traumatic to the woman if the father of the child either opposes the abortion or insists on it. Some men do not want their wives or girlfriends to have an abortion, and have even gone to court to try to stop it. Doctors have reported that some men oppose an abortion even when they do not intend to support the woman financially or emotionally. More often, the man is silent because he feels he has to "protect" the woman, or he feels it's up to her to make the final decision. Sometimes after the abortion has been performed, the couple realizes that neither partner really wanted it to occur.

Sometimes it is the man who suffers from guilt, and occasionally men have suffered temporary impotence. On the other hand, a man may refuse to take any responsibility for the decision, especially if the pregnancy is the result of a casual relationship or one-night stand.

An abortion can also affect the parent-child relationship even if the woman is not a minor. What the parents want the woman to do sometimes conflicts with what she wants to do. Even when everybody agrees that an abortion is the right choice, the parents may feel they have failed in some way. For example, they may feel they have failed to instill moral values in their daughter, or they have failed to provide her with birth control information.

Friends, ministers, doctors, social workers, and counselors are sometimes supportive of a woman who is faced with deciding whether or not to have an abortion. There are also times when these people can cause her further stress. They may condemn her for considering an abortion, especially if it conflicts with their religious beliefs. A *New York Times*/CBS News poll done in 1979 found that a majority of Americans approved of legal abortion. But they did not approve of them for friends. The survey asked, "Would you approve of someone you know having an abortion?" About 32 percent of the Protestants and 27 percent of the Catholics polled said yes; 37 percent of the Protestants and 44 percent of the Catholics said no. A high proportion—25 percent—of both groups said, "It all depends."

Regardless of the age of the woman or the circumstances surrounding an unwanted pregnancy, having an abortion is not easy. In his statement to Congress in 1974, Dr. Samuel Barr said, "I will dismiss as nonsense the premise that you have that anyone . . . patient, physicians, social worker, clergyman, takes abortion lightly. I further dismiss as nonsense the premise that anyone 'favors abortion.'"

THREE

The Sides

The Supporters of Choice

Historically and legally, the fetus has not been viewed as a "person." This is the way that people supporting a woman's right to choose abortion view it; to them, abortion is not the same as taking a life. They believe that the pregnant woman has a right to choose whether to have an abortion or not.

Daniel C. Maguire, a professor of moral theology at Marquette University, who asked to see an aborted fetus between six and nine weeks old, wrote that the "quantity was so little that I could have hidden it if I had taken it into my hand and made a fist. It was impressive to realize that I was holding in the cup what many people think to be the legal and moral peer of a woman." Some people who favor choice, however, seem to overstate their position by calling the fetus "a mass of tissue," a "parasite," "almost valueless," or "a bit of vegetating unborn matter."

Trying to decide when the fetus becomes a "person" often presents the choice advocates with a moral dilemma. The majority of choice supporters are in the middle of the spectrum. They support legal abortion, but they do not necessarily support it at all stages of the pregnancy. Generally they draw the line at the point when it's possible that the fetus can survive outside the womb. They also would not necessarily have an abortion themselves.

The majority of Americans, according to a wide variety of polls, support legal abortion. In a 1985 *Newsweek* poll, 76 percent of those surveyed agreed that abortion should be legal—21 percent in all cases and 55 percent in some cases. These percentages are often higher when the pollster asks people about specific instances, for example, aborting a fetus with severe retardation. A wide variety of professional, women's, and religious groups—such as the National Organization for Women (NOW), the American Medical Association, Planned Parenthood, the American Bar Association, and the National Association for the Repeal of Abortion Laws (NARAL)—also endorse legal abortion.

A major misunderstanding regarding abortion is that people think that all religious groups oppose it. This is not true—the majority of churches and religious organizations in the United States support legal abortion. These include the United Presbyterian Church, the United Church of God, Church of the Brethren, Lutheran Baptist Church in America, the Unitarian Universalist Association, the American Baptist Church, the National Council of Jewish Women, Presbyterian Church in the U.S., Reformed Church in America, American Friends Service Committee, and the Episcopal Church. Within religious groups, the main opposition to abortion comes from the Roman Catholic Church and the fundamentalist Protestant churches.

In general, most churches recognize that abortion is not desirable, but that sometimes it is the best step when moral values clash. For example, the Mormon Church calls abortion a "sinful practice." Yet abortion is permissible to Mormons in "rare cases where . . . the life or good health of the mother is seriously endangered or where the pregnancy was caused by rape and produces serious emotional trauma in the mother."

In 1972, before abortion was legalized, the United Methodist Church endorsed legal abortion. The Methodists passed a resolution that stated, "We believe that a profound regard for unborn human life must be weighed alongside an equally profound regard for fully formed personhood, particularly when the physical, mental and emotional health of the pregnant woman and her family show reason to be seriously threatened."

The advocates of legal abortion do not all agree on when abortion is acceptable. As one woman said, "Abortion isn't 'right,' but it is sometimes necessary." According to a poll taken in 1980 by the National Opinion Research Center, 90 percent of Americans are in favor of legal abortions if the woman's health is at stake. Even the Catholic Church, which opposes abortion, makes a distinction between direct and indirect abortions. An indirect abortion occurs when the fetus is killed in the process of saving the mother. For example, if a pregnant woman has cancer of the uterus, the uterus has to be removed to save the woman's life. The fetus, of course, dies, but the death of the fetus is not the goal of the operation, so it is considered morally acceptable. Similarly, it is acceptable to the Catholic Church to end an ectopic pregnancy, in which the fetus develops not in the womb but in the fallopian tubes. Of course, many theologians feel it is necessary to try to save the fetus if there is any chance at all.

About 83 percent of Americans approve of abortion in cases of rape. A woman with a bumper sticker reading ABORTION IS MURDER said she makes two exceptions: to save the woman's life and to end a pregnancy caused by rape. Yet it is relatively rare for a woman to abort because she is pregnant as a result of a rape. Generally, a woman who seeks medical assistance following a rape is given a D & C straightaway, which removes any possibility of pregnancy.

About 83 percent of Americans approve of abortions when the fetus is abnormal or when it is likely to suffer from a disability later in life. An abortion of an abnormal fetus frequently arouses heated debate, and it raises a serious moral question—Is a person "unfit" for society just because he or she suffers from a disability or mental retardation?

Significantly smaller percentages of Americans approve of abortion for social reasons, or what are called "soft" reasons. About 52 percent approve of an abortion if the family is poor, 48 percent if the woman is single, 47 percent if she is married and doesn't want more children, and 42 percent for any reason. Even so, it is for "soft" reasons that most abortions are performed.⌋

⌈Abortions done because of medical reasons, rape, or fetal defects are a small percentage of all abortions performed today⌋ That was even true over twenty years ago, when Alice S. Rossi wrote her essay "Abortion Laws and Their Victims." In it she stated,

> Few women who seek abortions have been exposed to German measles or taken thalidomide and hence fear a deformed fetus; few have serious heart or liver conditions that constitute a threat to their life if they carried the pregnancy to term; fewer still have been raped by a stranger or by their own father. The majority of women who seek abortions do so because they find themselves with unwelcome or unwanted pregnancies; abortion is a last-resort birth-control measure when preventive techniques have failed or have not been used. It is the situation *of not wanting a child* that covers the main rather than the exceptional abortion situation.

⌈Not only in the United States, but also throughout the world, whether the abortions are legal or illegal, the vast majority of them are performed for social or economic reasons. These reasons include poverty, poor housing, divorce, illegitimacy, enough children, and drug addiction.② They also include a woman's personal goals and needs, for example, an opportunity for a promotion, a company transfer, or finishing school. There are many cases in which only the pregnant woman, say the choice supporters, can judge whether or not an abortion is right or wrong for her at that time.

Those who do approve of abortion for "soft" reasons feel the quality of life the child will have is an important factor to consider. They believe that it is morally wrong to bring an unwanted child into the world. They argue that it is not only unfair to the woman to make her bear an unwanted child, but it is unfair to the child as well. There are many studies showing that unwanted children are often abused or abandoned or live lives of poverty and frustration. Unwanted children are more likely than wanted children to become juvenile delinquents and to become poor parents themselves. "Why bring unwanted children into a world that is in the midst of a population explosion?" ask the groups in favor of choice.

The groups who support choice do not view adoption as a solution to abortion. They point out that thousands of minority, older, or disabled children are currently awaiting adoption. They also note that 93 percent of women faced with an unexpected pregnancy consider only two choices: keeping the child or aborting.

There are many who argue that abortion is a woman's right—pure and simple. They say that that right has been denied because men have made the laws regulating abortion. Philosopher Judith Thomson argues that carrying a fetus is like lending a body to a person in need of it. But, she says, "Having a right to life does not guarantee either a right to be given the use of, or a right to be allowed continuous use of, another person's body—even if one needs it for life itself."

Prochoice lobbyist Barbara Shack says that women are powerless if they cannot control their own pregnancies.

According to a recent survey of women in California by University of San Diego sociologist Kristin Luker, the average prochoice advocate is forty-four years old, married to a professional, has a college degree, has no strong religious ties, and works outside the home. This woman has a work role closely connected to her self-identity, so she feels that women have to control their pregnancies in order to control their careers. Historically, pregnancy has restricted women's work opportunities.

Feminist and civil rights leader Flo Kennedy makes the pithy comment that "if men could become pregnant, abortion would be a sacrament."

A very strong argument put forth by the prochoice groups is that women have always resorted to abortions —legally or illegally—for unwanted pregnancies. It is estimated that seven out of ten women with such pregnancies would have illegal abortions if legal ones were banned. According to a *Newsweek* poll completed in 1985, 88 percent of Americans believe that women would have illegal abortions if legal ones were not available.

There is no denying that illegal abortions are dangerous. They often cause severe bleeding and infections. They sometimes cause sterility and even death. In the decade before abortion was legalized, as many as fifteen women were brought into large city hospitals each night suffering from complications arising from illegal abortions.

The number of illegal abortions carried out in the United States before abortion was made legal is unknown. It is impossible to obtain accurate statistics because neither the woman nor the abortionist is likely to admit that an abortion took place. The estimates presented range from 200,000 to as many as 1,200,000 illegal abortions performed per year. The choice supporters quote the high figures, while the antichoice groups quote low figures—each using the figures to support their own case. It is estimated that only one-third of the illegal abortions were performed by doctors, many of whom were "has beens," alcoholics, or inept.

What *is* known about illegal abortions is that thousands of women died from complications caused by them. In the 1930s in the United States, there were about 8,000 such deaths every year. The number of deaths dropped each decade afterward because of improved medical care, including better antibiotics. Yet it is certain that even with today's antibiotics, illegal abortions would cause women great pain, suffering, and even death.

There are many people who are opposed to abortion for themselves for moral or ethical reasons, but who support the fact that abortion is legal. One woman who heads a medical clinic says,

> I can see both sides of the issue. I can still remember when abortion was illegal. I attended a small, rural college in Pennsylvania. A friend of mine became pregnant in her senior year. She did not want to get married, and it would have ruined her life to have had a child at

that time. She had an illegal abortion in Pittsburgh and almost died as a result. But my son is adopted and I'm so glad his mother did not have an abortion. Making abortions illegal won't stop women from having them, however.

Supporters of a woman's right to choose do not take abortion as lightly as anti-abortionists often claim. The feminist Simone de Beauvoir wrote about abortion in her classic book *The Second Sex*. She believed that a woman seeking an abortion is "divided against herself. . . . For if it is not true that abortion is murder, it still cannot be considered in the same light as a mere contraceptive technique; an event has taken place that is a definite beginning, the progress of which is to be stopped."

It is the abortion that the right-to-life groups feel must be stopped. They are working very actively to achieve that goal.

The Opponents of Abortion

The people who oppose legal abortion are in the minority in the United States; according to a 1985 *Newsweek* poll, they make up 22 percent of the population. They call themselves "right-to-life supporters" or describe themselves as "prolife," while others label them "antichoice."

Among the anti-abortion groups, which are generally politically conservative or right wing, many are extremely active. They include the National Right to Life Committee; March for Life; Alternatives to Abortion; National Conference of Catholic Bishops; the American

Life Lobby; the Pro-Life Action League, founded by Joseph M. Scheidler, a former monk; and the Moral Majority, recently renamed Liberty Federation, founded in 1979 by Reverend Jerry Falwell, a Baptist minister from Virginia.

As noted earlier, these groups oppose abortion because they believe a fetus is a person, and that aborting it is murder. They place the start of life at conception. Said Dr. Jerome Lejeune, Medical College of Paris, "Life has a very, very long history, but each individual has a very neat beginning, the moment of conception."

The anti-abortionists believe that the fetus is entitled to protection of life in accordance with the American Constitution. They argue that the fetus's right to life outweighs the woman's right to choose whether or not to have a child. They dismiss the argument that it is acceptable to destroy the fetus because it cannot live outside the womb.

President Ronald Reagan personally believes that a fetus is a human being. Asked to comment on the conflicting opinions about the start of life, he said, "If we don't know, then shouldn't we morally opt on the side that it is life? If you came upon an immobile body and could not determine whether it was dead or alive, you would consider it alive until somebody could prove it was dead. We should do the same thing with regard to abortion."

There are other reasons why the anti-abortionists want to prohibit abortion. They feel they are preserving the family and the sanctity of motherhood. Kristin Luker, University of San Diego sociologist, found in a recent California survey that the typical anti-abortionist woman is forty-four years old, a housewife, religious, and a high school graduate. Of the 37 percent who do work outside the home, most are in traditionally female jobs, such as nursing.

Phyllis Schlafly, who headed StopERA, a group opposed to the Equal Rights Amendment, and the anti-abortion group Eagle Forum, organized many rallies at which women demanded the rights "not to take a job, to keep our babies, and to be supported by our husbands."

Because many anti-abortionists are housewives or religious leaders, they have the time to devote to their cause. They are very active politically despite the fact that they have not been involved in politics before.

The majority of anti-abortionists also object to abortion because they feel it promotes sexual activity. They oppose premarital sex and sex education in the schools.

The anti-abortionists charge that women have abortions for what they see as "trivial" reasons, such as financial strain. They also feel that abortion services are becoming big business and that money is a motivation for some of those who are in favor of abortion.

"Every child is wanted—by someone," contend those opposing choice. They view adoption as a logical alternative to abortion.

Those opposed to abortion on request contend that legalized abortion will lead to a decline in our society and our morality. They feel it destroys the dignity of men and women and reduces them to "expendable things." Novelist Walker Percy wrote, "True legalized abortion—a million and a half fetuses flushed down the disposal each year in this country—is yet another banal atrocity in a century where atrocities have become commonplace."

In the opinion of the anti-abortionists, liberal abortion laws will destroy our society and lead the country to become like Nazi Germany, where mass murder took place. Those favoring choice, however, point out that Nazi Germany had strict anti-abortion laws. Abortion was penalized severely unless there was a suspicion of a congenital defect which they tried to attribute to a non-Aryan parent.

Many anti-abortionists feel that the legalization of abortion can lead to euthanasia. That is the view of Dr. Carolyn F. Gerster, former president of the National Right to Life Committee. During the Senate hearings on the "human life" law, she said, "If one is prepared to give the woman the unrestricted right to kill her unborn daughter, one had better be prepared to some day give the daughter the unrestricted right to kill the aged mother. Euthanasia has followed abortion as night follows the day." The prochoice groups say that her charge is ridiculous and that euthanasia has not occurred in countries where abortion has been legal for decades.

Anti-abortionists also claim that the aborted fetuses are used for bizarre experiments. That charge, according to Planned Parenthood of America, is unfounded. In the past, notably in Finland in the 1960s, there were hideous experiments on living fetuses, but they were not funded by the United States nor supported by the United States in any way.

Although they are in the minority, the anti-abortionists feel it is their right—even their duty—to work to ban abortion. Catholic philosopher Daniel Callahan says that "every movement of social reform in the United States—the enactment of laws protecting trade unions, the black civil-rights movement, for instance—began as minority movements, often the object of extreme hostility on the part of the majority."

The Religious Connection

Theologians say that opposition to abortion is rooted in church doctrine and comes from the Tenth Commandment, which says, "Thou shall not kill." They point out that there are no clear-cut statements about abortion in the Bible.

In recent years, according to the National Opinion Research Center, there has been growing opposition to abortion from the fundamentalist churches. But it's the hierarchy of the Roman Catholic Church that has been in the forefront of the anti-abortion movement. Barbara Lindheim is a researcher at the Alan Guttmacher Institute, which is a nonprofit planning organization that conducts research and is affiliated with Planned Parenthood. She said, "Without the institutional backing of the Catholic Church, the prolife movement would be a much less visible force. There is no other single institution that has gotten involved in such a visible way. The church has provided money, local organization, shock troops, and even mimeo machines." Church officials encouraged members of the congregation to join such groups as the National Right to Life (NRTL) organization and provided meeting places for local chapters.

The Catholic Bishops' Committee for Pro-Life Activities set up the National Committee for a Human Life Amendment, a lobbying group, in 1973. Two years later it published the "Pastoral Plan for Pro-life Activities." The guide gave local churches advice on how to work to have laws passed to restrict abortion and how to campaign against legislators who support legal abortion.

There are hundreds of state and local branches of the National Right to Life Committee and similar organizations. They have worked hard to elect legislators opposed to abortion and to defeat anyone who supports abortion rights in any way. The Church has recently been charged with providing funds to support anti-abortion activities and to help elect anti-abortionists to legislative bodies. This activity is in opposition to the principle in the Constitution of "separation of church and state." Frequently, money is collected outside churches to donate to anti-abortionists running for office.

The Catholic Church has put particular pressure on particular Catholic candidates, such as the Democrat's 1980 vice-presidential candidate Geraldine Ferraro. Ferraro is personally opposed to abortion but not in favor of banning it. Wherever she spoke during her campaign, she was picketed by anti-abortionists.

Actually, the percentage of lay Catholics who support legal abortion is almost as high as the percentage of

Protestants. In fact, a 1977 National Opinion Research Center survey found that 66 percent of Catholics supported abortions in cases of a defective fetus; 76 percent when the woman's health is in danger. That does not mean, however, that they would have an abortion themselves or that they would support an abortion for "soft" reasons.

There are Catholic organizations devoted to protecting legal abortion because they do not want to impose their religious beliefs on society or force women to resort to illegal abortions. Among such organizations are Catholics for a Free Choice, which counts priests and nuns as members, and the Vatican 24. The Vatican 24 are nuns who support legal abortion and who have been threatened with expulsion from their religious order. They signed a statement asking the Catholic Church to reconsider its stand on abortion. They have stated, "The Vatican is consciously choosing to ignore women's experiences; minimize women's lives; trivialize women's struggles to make difficult decisions on reproductive rights; and to divide women against women."

Catholic theologian Daniel Maguire wrote an article in *Ms.* magazine in December 1984 in which he asked, "Why is the Vatican comparably sure that while there may be *just* wars with incredible slaughter, there can be no *just* abortions?"

The fundamentalist Protestant groups and interdenominational groups, such as the Moral Majority, have been just as active in opposing abortion as the Catholic

Church. They have also employed similar methods of opposition.

All of the anti-abortion groups have set as their main goal the overturning of the Supreme Court's decisions —*Roe* v. *Wade* and *Doe* v. *Bolton*. It was these two decisions that made abortion legal.

FOUR

The Supreme Court Decision

The Supreme Court made abortion legal nationally on January 22, 1973, when it handed down two decisions: *Roe* v. *Wade* and *Doe* v. *Bolton*. Those decisions limited a state's right to ban abortion. In effect, the Court made abortion legal until the fetus is viable, or capable of living outside the womb.

The more famous case, *Roe* v. *Wade*, began in 1970. A woman, who called herself Jane Roe, challenged a 100-year-old Texas law forbidding abortion except to save the life of the mother. She was unmarried, twenty-one years old, a high school dropout, and divorced mother of a daughter. As a result of a gang rape, she became pregnant. She was working as a waitress, and she was afraid of losing her job because of her pregnancy.

At the time, "Jane" would have been able to obtain a legal abortion in a handful of states that had reformed their abortion laws, including California. In 1969, California had made abortion legal in cases of rape, incest, and danger to the health of the woman. Jane, however, did not have the money to go there, so she tried to obtain financial aid through a lawyer. He put her in touch with two lawyers who were looking for a strong case to challenge Texas's abortion law. When Jane went to see them, they agreed that her case was what they had been looking for.

Jane agreed to test the constitutionality of Texas's abortion law. She brought suit against Henry Wade, the district attorney of Dallas County, who was responsible for enforcing the law in the area where she lived. The case was tried in a Dallas federal district court, and Jane won it. The court struck down the abortion law.

Texas appealed the decision; while the case was in appeal, the abortion law remained in effect. That meant that Jane could not legally have an abortion in Texas. Jane turned down her attorney's offer to pay for an abortion in California because she did not want to damage the case. She gave birth to her child and gave it up for adoption before the appeal made its way to the Supreme Court in 1973.

In *Doe* v. *Bolton,* a woman challenged the abortion law in Georgia which compared to the laws in Texas could be considered liberal. If Jane had lived in Georgia, she would have been able to obtain a legal abortion. Georgia had reformed its abortion law, making abortion legal in cases in which the mother's health was at stake, in instances of rape, and in cases involving an abnormal fetus. The law required the following conditions be met: that the abortion be done in an accredited hospital, that it be approved by a board, that the doctor's opinion be confirmed by two other doctors, and that the woman be a resident of the state. The woman calling herself Doe was pregnant, married, poor, and twenty-two years old. She had given birth to three children: Two of them had been placed in a foster home, and one had been put up for adoption. Like *Roe* v. *Wade,* Doe's case worked its way up to the Supreme Court.

Both Georgia and Texas defended their laws by arguing that the fetus is a person from the moment of conception (when the egg and sperm unite). The fetus, they argued, is entitled to protection under Section 1 of the Fourteenth Amendment to the U.S. Constitution which states: " . . . No State shall make or enforce any law which shall abridge the privileges or immunities of citizens of the United States; nor shall any State deprive a person of life, liberty, or property, without due process of law; nor deny to any person within its jurisdiction the equal protection of the laws."

The lawyers for Roe and Doe argued that the abortion laws abridged their clients' right of personal privacy, which was also protected by the Constitution. They further argued that historically a fetus was not considered a person in the eyes of the law. For example, causing a woman to miscarry does not constitute murder, but assault.

In both cases, the Supreme Court of the United States ruled against the particular states. In *Roe* v. *Wade* the Court ruled that the fetus is not a person and is not entitled to Constitutional protection. Justice Blackmun wrote the decision for the majority. He said,

The Constitution does not define "person" in so many words. . . . The word person, as used in the Fourteenth Amendment, does not include the unborn. . . . We need not resolve the difficult question of when life begins. When those trained in the respective disciplines of medicine, philosophy, and theology are unable to arrive at any consensus, the judiciary, at this point in the development of man's knowledge, is not in a position to speculate as to the answer. It should be sufficient to note briefly the wide divergence of thinking on this most sensitive and difficult question.

The majority opinion also stated that a woman has the right to have an abortion in order to prevent a "distressful life and future." That element was based on the Constitution's guarantee of personal liberty, which the Court said included a woman's personal decision to end or continue her pregnancy.

In *Doe* v. *Bolton,* the Supreme Court reiterated its Roe decision. It noted that a woman's health—in a very broad sense—is a factor in the decision whether to have an abortion or not. But the Court, as it had done in *Roe,* stated, "a pregnant woman does not have an absolute constitutional right to an abortion on her demand." The Court voided Georgia's requirements that an abortion be done in a hospital, that it be approved by a hospital committee, that the need for an abortion be confirmed by two licensed doctors, and that the woman be a resident of the state.

Justices William H. Rehnquist and Byron R. White disagreed, or dissented, with both decisions. Writing his minority opinion, Rehnquist, who became Chief Justice in 1986, stated that he believed that the Court lacked any "reason or authority" for its decision in favor of abortion.

Justice White was critical of the Court's decisions, and he wrote that the Court valued the "convenience of the pregnant mother more than the continued existence and development of the life or potential life which she carries."

The decisions in *Roe* v. *Wade* and *Doe* v. *Bolton* voided the abortion laws in forty-four states besides Texas and Georgia. Four states—Hawaii, Alaska, Washington, and New York—had already made abortion legal. The year after the Supreme Court legalized abortion nationally, about 750,000 were performed.

Yet, as noted earlier, the Court's decisions in *Roe* v. *Wade* and *Doe* v. *Bolton* did not allow "abortion on demand," as many anti-abortionists charged. The Court did not completely take away the state's right to restrict or govern abortion. In order to ensure safe medical practices, the court gave the states the right to regulate abortions during the second trimester. For example, it gave states the right to require that a second-trimester abortion be done by a doctor in a licensed clinic.

In *Roe* v. *Wade,* the Supreme Court also gave the states the right to "place increasing restrictions on abortion as the period of pregnancy lengthens." It allowed the states to forbid abortions during the third trimester except to save the life or health of the mother. It allowed the states this right because it found that the fetus can be viable, or capable of a "meaningful life" outside the womb, during the last three months of a pregnancy. The Court said, "With respect to the State's important and legitimate interest in potential life, the 'compelling' point is at viability. . . . If the State is interested in protecting fetal life after viability, it may go so far as to proscribe abortion during that period except when it is necessary to preserve the life or health of the mother."

The Supreme Court stated, "Viability is usually placed at about seven months (28 weeks) but may occur earlier, even at 24 weeks." Since then, there have been many claims that younger and younger fetuses should be considered viable because of technological advances in fetal care and modern incubators. It's true that premature infants have a good chance of survival at twenty-six weeks, and more are saved these days than used to be. But Dr. Richard Stavis, who directs a neonatal unit at the Bryn Mawr Hospital in Bryn Mawr, Pennsylvania, says the likelihood of survival before twenty-four weeks is close to zero and that at twenty-six weeks the odds are still very low because the fetal lungs are not developed. Those infants who do survive generally have serious abnormalities.

Nevertheless, with advances in medical science it is likely that the time of viability will occur earlier in the pregnancy. Many experts on the Constitution feel that the Supreme Court's *Roe* v. *Wade* decision will then be obsolete because a viable fetus is generally viewed legally as the same as an infant. Still, the Court did not say that the states had to outlaw abortions after viability.

Although the Supreme Court's legalizing abortion was approved by the majority of Americans, there were many people who were appalled. A newspaper editorial in the *St. Louis Review* said that the Court's ruling "may well unleash an era of carnage and slaughter which could quickly eclipse the bloody record of Hitler's Germany." Although many anti-abortionists were stunned by the Supreme Court's decision, in fact, the Court was following a trend toward abortion reform. It was not leading the way.

FIVE

Leading up to *Roe*

When the Supreme Court of the United States legalized abortion in 1973, many people were surprised and called it a "bolt from the blue." In reality, the Court decision followed on the heels of a movement to reform abortion laws that was having an effect all over the country.

As early as 1962, the American Law Institute, a nonprofit organization, issued guidelines for more liberal abortion laws. It recommended allowing abortions when the mother's health was in jeopardy, when the pregnancy was the result of rape or incest, when the mother was under the age of sixteen, and when it was probable that the fetus would be abnormal.

The American Law Institute was not alone in lobbying for reform of the abortion laws. Many organizations passed resolutions in favor of abortion reform. They included the American Bar Association, the American

Association of University Women, the American College of Obstetricians and Gynecologists, the Women's Medical Association, the American Public Health Association, Planned Parenthood, the National Organization for Women (NOW) and Zero Population Growth. In 1967, the American Medical Association voted overwhelmingly in favor of liberalized abortion laws, although a century earlier, it had led the fight to make abortion illegal.

By the late 1960s several polls showed that a majority of Americans supported legal abortion. A Lou Harris poll, taken in 1969 for *Time* magazine, revealed that 64 percent of those polled were in favor of legal abortion. By 1967, thirteen states had passed laws based on the American Law Institute's recommendations.

The movement to reform the abortion laws was spurred by several factors.

• The abortion laws were generally not enforced and were no deterrent to abortion.

• In practice, hospitals across the country stretched the laws and performed abortions that did not conform to them literally.

• Poor women who resorted to illegal abortions were discriminated against by the laws.

• The laws were based on religious and ethical values that were not universally shared.

• The laws were viewed by many as an infringement of a woman's rights.

Lack of Enforcement

It was no secret that abortion laws were not enforced. It was all but impossible to obtain evidence of an abortion, as the fetus was always quickly destroyed. It was also difficult to get witnesses to testify; doctors were unwilling to go to court, and the woman involved was certainly unwilling. Most important, a very large segment of the population disagreed with the laws, so law enforcement officials tended to look the other way. Similarly, during Prohibition, alcoholic beverages were illegal but widely available.

Before the legalization of abortion, abortions were allowed for "therapeutic" reasons in order to protect the woman's health. Whether "therapeutic" was defined broadly or narrowly was up to the doctor and the hospital. There were enormous differences between what different doctors and hospitals labeled as "therapeutic," especially after medical advances had made pregnancy less and less dangerous. By the 1950s, many hospitals had established boards of doctors who had to approve the abortion. Abortion had moved beyond being just a medical issue into the realm of moral, personal, and political issues.

According to a study by Robert Hall done in 1965, there were no abortions and over 24,000 deliveries at one hospital. In another hospital there was one abortion for every thirty-six births. He noted, "Abortion practices vary not only from hospital to hospital but also from . . . doctor to doctor [in] the same hospital. The victim of all this confusion is, of course, the American female. Even if she has a legitimate reason for therapeutic abortion she must find Doctor X in hospital Y with policy Z in order to have it done."

During hearings to reform the abortion law in California, doctors admitted that abortions were taking place that were not "legal" if interpreted according to the letter of the state law. That is, the abortions were performed not necessarily to save lives, but they were justified as necessary to save the woman's mental health. The same thing was obviously happening elsewhere, too, and it was dramatically revealed in a well-publicized case in which a woman named Sherri Finkbine sought an abortion in Arizona.

Sherri Finkbine took thalidomide, an antinausea drug that her husband had purchased in Europe. At the time she was pregnant with her fifth child. Then she found out that thalidomide was linked with extremely severe abnormalities in the fetus. After struggling with her worries, she decided to have an abortion. She was given her doctor's assurance that the hospital board would approve of an abortion in her case. She was scheduled to have the operation, but it never took place—at least not in Arizona. Because she was concerned about the effects of thalidomide on pregnant women, she had told the press her story. The papers broke it on the day before her abortion was scheduled, and the hospital board refused to allow her to have an abortion.

Sherri Finkbine finally went to Sweden to have a legal abortion, and there she learned that the fetus was badly deformed. Her dramatic story made national headlines. The anti-abortionists criticized and harassed her, but they were in the minority. According to a Gallup poll, 50 percent of those surveyed supported her decision to have an abortion and 16 percent had no opinion.

About the same time, an epidemic of German measles caused many women to ask for therapeutic abortions. If a woman has German measles during the first three months of her pregnancy, there is the possibility that the fetus will suffer from congenital problems. In states where abortion was illegal, abortions done because of a defective fetus were defended on grounds that they were necessary to preserve the woman's mental health. Doctors began to lobby in favor of legal abortion because they wanted a free hand to decide whether or not to perform an abortion, especially in "borderline" cases. Although it was extremely rare for doctors to be prosecuted for performing an illegal abortion in a hospital, they did not want to risk being confronted with criminal charges or expensive lawsuits.

Poor Women Faced Discrimination

It was no secret that women with the money or connections were able to get abortions that were safer than those that poor women received. The well-to-do were able to pay for abortions, sometimes performed by doctors who called the abortion "therapeutic." Wealthy women were also more likely to be able to plead psychiatric problems as a reason for a legal abortion. If they were well off they could simply travel to countries like Japan or Sweden, where abortion was legal. Poor women were at the mercy of back-alley abortionists and suffered far greater complications from illegal abortions. In his book *Abortion and the Law,* Dr. Harold Rosen wrote, "The difference between having an abortion or a child . . . is the difference between having one to three hundred dollars and knowing the right person or being without funds and the right contacts."

Religious/Ethical Conflicts

The abortion laws were based on religious and ethical principles. These principles were not shared by everyone. It was a common, but mistaken, notion that all religious groups opposed abortion. The majority of religious groups do not oppose it and do not place the beginning of human life at the moment of conception. The main opposition to abortion comes from the Roman Catholic Church. More lay Catholics however, disagree than agree with Church policy.

In a 1969 Lou Harris poll taken for *Time* magazine, 60 percent of the Catholics questioned agreed that having an abortion was up to the woman and her doctor and not up to the legal system. On the whole, the survey found that 64 percent of Americans believed an abortion was a personal matter.

A Woman's Right

At the start of the women's movement, when feminists were demanding equal rights for women, few demanded the right to abortion. Eventually, however, they said that without the right to control their own bodies, their other rights were all but destroyed. They believed that in order to control their careers, they had to control their pregnancies. Employers were reluctant to hire women of child-bearing age. It was seen as a waste of time and effort to train a woman who might leave the company if she became pregnant. In the 1950s and 1960s, it was not as common for women to return to work after having a child as it is today. Women made up about 26 percent of the paid work force in 1950 and by 1981 they made up 43 percent of it. In the late 1980s, more mothers work than don't.

Eventually women began to demand the right to legal abortion. In 1967, the National Organization for Women (NOW) began its campaign for nationwide abortion reform. NOW lost several members who were against the call for legal abortion. But NOW founder Betty Friedan said, "The women speaking up passionately for it were not only the young women, but the square, middle-aged housewife types from Indiana and points south."

As they had done in their fight to win the vote, women went out into the streets to fight for the right to an abortion. They staged marches all over the country demanding equal rights and abortion rights. In Detroit, they staged a funeral march for the women who died as a result of illegal abortions.

Women who had had illegal abortions began to speak out about them. They told about the horrors of abortions done without anesthetics in dirty hotel rooms or kitchens. They told about the pain, the psychological and emotional trauma, and the guilt over both the abortion and breaking the law. Doctors and nurses talked about the women who were admitted to the hospitals after botched abortions, women who still had coat hangers in their abdomens, women who had been burned by severe chemicals. In large city hospitals, up to fifteen patients a night were admitted for complications due to illegal or self-induced abortions, and often two or three were so badly injured they required intensive care.

In 1972, *Ms.* magazine published a petition signed

by fifty-two prominent women who admitted to having had an abortion. Thousands of readers responded by sending in their names. Along with the women's movement, a sexual revolution took place during the 1960s, a decade of great social change. The introduction of birth control pills accelerated the trend toward premarital sex. At the same time, the increase in divorces and the decline in marriage made sex outside marriage more and more common.

When it was introduced, the pill was thought to be the answer to unwanted pregnancy. It is 99 percent effective if used as prescribed. But in time, studies showed that it had serious side effects and that some women were unable to take it at all. These women had to use other methods of birth control, none 100 percent effective. Condoms, diaphragms, and foam are about 85 percent to 95 percent effective. IUDs are 97 percent effective, but often cause severe bleeding and cramps. Even sterilization is not guaranteed to be 100 percent effective; there are rare instances when it fails and pregnancy occurs. Abortion is a last resort when birth control fails.

As a result of all this, the movement to reform the abortion laws took root. It was one reflection of the many changes taking place in our society, particularly in regard to the role of women.

Liberalization by the States

By the end of the 1960s, several states had reformed their abortion laws, or the courts had nullified them. Colorado was the first (1967) and California, after its abortion law was challenged, was second.

In 1969, the Supreme Court of California, by a vote of four to three, ruled the state's 100-year-old abortion law invalid. It said that the phrase "necessary to preserve the life of the mother" was too vague and impossible for doctors to follow. In contrast, at about the same time, similar laws in Massachusetts and New Jersey were challenged, and the respective state courts found the same wording understandable and acceptable. This only hastened the reform movement.

In all, twenty states, including Delaware, Kansas, Oregon, North Carolina, Georgia, Florida, California, and New Mexico, had changed and liberalized their laws to some degree before the Supreme Court made abortion legal nationwide. Only four states had made all abortions legal, at least during the first trimester: Hawaii, New York, Washington, and Alaska.

Most of the state laws were based on the American Law Institute model, and allowed abortions to protect the life of the mother, to prevent damage to the mental and physical health of the woman, and to end pregnancies that were the result of rape or incest. But the laws were not uniform. For example, Missouri only liberalized the law to allow legal abortions in the event of rape.

The laws generally did not spell out what constituted a threat to the physical or mental health of the woman. That gave doctors great latitude in deciding whether or not to perform an abortion. More and more doctors came to believe that social problems were grounds for an abortion, as they had a bearing on the woman's mental state.

Most of the state laws permitted abortions of abnormal fetuses. California was a notable exception. When the state legislature was attempting to write a new abortion law, Ronald Reagan was governor. He threatened to veto the law if it allowed abortions for fetal abnormalities. The law was written banning such abortions, but doctors sometimes argued that carrying an abnormal fetus was a threat to the woman's mental health, making the abortion legal. Colorado and Maryland allowed abortions for fetal disorders if they were "grave and permanent," Georgia if there were no chances for correction, and North Carolina if the problem was serious. Doctors, of course, often differed on what was noncorrectable or serious.

The abortion laws also contained specific conditions. For example, some states, such as Georgia, only allowed abortions for state residents; New York and California did not restrict abortions this way. Colorado did not have a residency requirement, but doctors feared turning the state hospitals into "abortion mills," so they often turned down out-of-state women. Soon after the new abortion law was passed in Maryland, three hospitals in Baltimore (Sinai, Johns Hopkins, and the Greater Baltimore Medical Center) stopped doing abortions for nonresidents of the state.

The year before the Supreme Court made abortion legal nationwide, about 590,000 legal abortions were performed in the states with liberalized laws. The reason given for three-quarters of the legal abortions was to protect the mental health of the woman.

The women who lived in states with restrictive laws either traveled to a state where abortion was legal, or, if unable to afford travel, resorted to an illegal abortion.

The number of illegal abortions remained high, and many women suffered from complications caused by them.

Naturally, the fact that some women were able to receive legal abortions and some were not generated all types of protests and the initiation of many court cases challenging the restrictive laws. The abortion laws were challenged in at least twenty state courts; sometimes the laws were upheld and sometimes they were overthrown.

By the time *Roe* v. *Wade* and *Doe* v. *Bolton* finally worked their way up to the Supreme Court, the stage had been set for a change in abortion policies. When the Court struck down the states' abortion laws, and finally established nationwide policy permitting abortion, it was actually following the reform movement. Nevertheless, anti-abortionists went to work to try to overturn the Court's decisions.

SIX

Attempts to Overturn *Roe*

The Human Life Amendment

The opponents of abortion immediately moved into action when the Court handed down its *Roe* v. *Wade* decision. They launched a major effort to have the decision overturned by the passage of an amendment to the Constitution, declaring that the fetus is a "person." As a person, the fetus would be entitled to protection of life, liberty, and the pursuit of happiness. The amendment was labeled the "human life amendment" (HLA).

Within a week of the Supreme Court's legalization of abortion, the amendment was introduced in Congress by Senator James L. Buckley of New York. It was cosponsored by Senators Mark Hatfield of Oregon, Wallace F. Bennett of Utah, Carl T. Curtis of Nebraska,

Dewey F. Bartlett of Oklahoma, and Milton R. Young of North Dakota. The amendment stated that life begins when the egg implants itself in the uterus. Thus, it banned abortions except to save the life of the woman. It was the first of many human life amendments introduced over the years.

Typically, HLAs said something like: "The word *person* as used in the Constitution of the United States applies to all human beings irrespective of age, health, function or condition of dependency, including their unborn offspring at every stage of their biological development including fertilization."

The majority of the human life amendments banned abortion except to save the mother's life. There were some, however, that made no exceptions. One that was put forward is the "paramount right to life" amendment. It was endorsed by the anti-abortion organization March for Life. It read: "The paramount right to life is vested in each human being from the moment of fertilization without regard to age, health, or condition of dependency." Such an amendment does not address the conflict between a fetus's right to life and a woman's right to life. If a doctor sacrificed the life of the fetus to save the woman, would the doctor be subject to trial for manslaughter or murder?

If passed, it's possible that a human life amendment would have serious legal consequences. Would an HLA stating that life begins at conception make birth control methods like the IUD illegal? An IUD is generally believed to induce abortion, since it seems to work by preventing the implantation of a fertilized egg in the uterus. Would an HLA make investigations of miscarriages mandatory to ensure that an abortion had not taken place? Those questions would probably be left up to the courts to answer.

In 1975, the U.S. Commission on Civil Rights issued a report on the human life amendments, which was very critical of the possible repercussions should an HLA be passed. It charged that an HLA would interfere with the First Amendment, which guarantees freedom of religion, because not all religious groups place the beginning of life at conception or implantation.

The U.S. Commission on Civil Rights also stated that the HLA would "create chaos" within the legal system. By defining the fetus as a person, an HLA would affect tax laws, property laws, and criminal laws: If a pregnant woman is assaulted and miscarries, is the attacker guilty of murder or manslaughter? If the fetus is a person, can it be listed as a dependent on income tax returns?

In response to the report, anti-abortion members of Congress pushed through a bill forbidding the U.S. Commission on Civil Rights to issue more reports on abortion.

Because of the tremendous implications of an HLA, none of the twenty-four that have been introduced in Congress has ever come close to passing. It is important to note, however, that it is very difficult for any constitutional amendment to pass, because the parliamentary process is so complicated. After an amendment is introduced in Congress, it is sent to a committee. The committee then studies it and decides whether or not to send it out to the floor for a vote by the entire legislative house. If it goes to the floor, it takes a two-thirds vote for Congress to pass it. Then it has to be approved by three-fourths of the states before it goes into effect. The entire process usually takes years.

The Constitution does provide a second method of passing an amendment. It gives the states the right to call for a constitutional convention. Several states passed resolutions calling for a constitutional convention on the abortion issue before 1980. None have done so since, and seventeen more states are needed before such a convention could be held. Never in the history of the United States has an amendment been passed at a constitutional convention. It is a method of creating laws that many lawyers fear would cause incredible problems because it is untested.

The human life amendments were sent to the Senate Judiciary Subcommittee, chaired by Senator Birch Bayh from Indiana. It was up to the Judiciary Subcommittee to hold or release the amendments. To help the committee make a decision, hearings were held on the abortion issue. During the hearings, there were many people who testified for or against a human life amendment.

Among those who spoke in favor of the HLA were Roman Catholic bishops. They called the *Roe* decision the "worst mistake in the Court's history."

Testifying against the HLA was Bishop A. James Armstrong of the United Methodist Church. He said, "In continuity with past Christian teaching, we recognize tragic conflicts of life with life that may justify abortion."

After the hearings, the Senate Judiciary Subcommittee decided not to send an HLA to the floor. Senator Birch Bayh, who was personally opposed to abortion, stated, "I feel that we cannot and must not use the Constitution as an instrument for moral preference. . . . It is precisely in areas that are so intimate, where public attitudes are so deeply divided, both morally and religiously, that private choice can be defended. . . ." Because his Subcommittee failed to release a human life or states' rights amendment, Bayh was targetted by the anti-abortionists. They campaigned against him, and partly because of their efforts, he was defeated in his reelection bid in 1980.

The Life Amendment Political Action Committee (LAPAC) worked to defeat several incumbent legislators who had voted against an HLA. One person they succeeded in removing from office was Senator Frank Church of Idaho.

Despite little congressional support of a human life amendment, new ones have been continually introduced in both houses of Congress. Over the years, Congress heard hundreds and hundreds of pages of testimony on both sides of the issue. None of the testimony apparently changed anyone's mind.

The States' Rights Amendment

When the human life amendments failed to pass Congress, the anti-abortionists came up with an alternative—a states' rights amendment. A typical states' rights amendment read: "Nothing in this Constitution shall bar any state or territory or the District of

Columbia with regard to any area over which it has jurisdiction, from allowing, regulating, or prohibiting the practice of abortion."

Like an HLA, a states' rights amendment would have serious effects. If passed, it would once again leave it up to the states to regulate abortion. This would mean a return to the way abortion was regulated before the Supreme Court legalized it nationwide. Women in some states would have the option of a legal abortion in their own state, and women in other states would not. Some fetuses would be protected and some would not. That method, say opponents of a states' rights amendment, has been tried and found inadequate.

Part of the appeal of the states' rights amendment was that it would have allowed Congress to avoid the issue of abortion. The problem could be dumped back into the laps of the state legislators. Both political parties, however, found themselves back in the midst of the debate when abortion became an issue during the presidential election of 1976.

The presidential candidates—Republican Gerald Ford and Democrat Jimmy Carter—were pressured by the right-to-life groups and by the media to take a stand on abortion. Ford, who was opposed to abortion, came out in favor of a states' rights amendment to regulate abortion. He was intensely criticized by both sides for his effort to take a middle-of-the-road position on abortion. Probably to his embarrassment, his wife Betty, who was noted for her honesty and boldness, came out in favor of nationwide legal abortion. She said that the Supreme Court decision allowed abortion to come "out of the backwoods and into the hospitals where it belongs."

Jimmy Carter was personally opposed to abortion as well. He said, "I don't think the government ought to do anything to encourage abortion. But I don't favor a Constitutional amendment on the subject." After Carter was elected, however, his administration attempted to curtail abortion. He appointed Joseph A. Califano, who opposed abortion, as Secretary of Health, Education, and Welfare (HEW), at what is now the Human Health Department (HHD). As head of HEW, he was instrumental in restricting abortions. For example, abortions were not performed in the Indian reservation health clinics or the sixty public health hospitals run by HEW. He also set up a committee to find alternatives to abortion. The committee concluded the alternatives were "suicide, motherhood, and some would add, madness. Consequently, there is some confusion, discomfort and cynicism greeting efforts to 'find' or 'emphasize' or 'identify' alternatives to abortion." Annoyed with the findings of the committee, Califano disbanded it.

While this was going on, poll after poll showed that at least 75 percent of Americans approved of legal abortion. At the same time, both human life amendments and states' rights amendments continued to come before Congress. To date, no amendments have been released by the Judiciary Subcommittee. Finally, Senator Buckley discovered a way to bypass the Judiciary Subcommittee, and managed to place a "right to life" amendment on the floor of the Senate. The amendment was debated, but instead of voting on it, the Senate voted forty-seven to forty to table it.

The Human Life Federalism Amendment

The efforts to overturn the Supreme Court's decision took a new turn in 1981 when Senator Orrin Hatch of Utah introduced a "Human Life Federalism" amendment (HLFA). It gave both Congress and the states the right to regulate abortion. It stated: "A right to abortion is not secured by this Constitution. The Congress and the several states have the concurrent power to restrict and prohibit abortions: provided, that a law of a State which is more restrictive than a law of Congress shall govern." Like the HLA and the states' rights amendments, the HLFA failed to pass. Had it passed, the HLFA would have overturned *Roe* v. *Wade* and would have meant a return to individual state laws. What was unique about the HLFA was that it reversed the usual procedure of having federal legislation take precedence over state laws.

More attempts were made to introduce an HLFA. One was introduced in 1983 by Senators Orrin Hatch and Thomas Eagleton of Missouri. It was released to the floor. For the first time, the Senate actually voted on an anti-abortion amendment. It was rejected by fifty votes to forty-nine. That was just eighteen votes short of the two-thirds majority needed to pass an amendment. Noted anti-abortionist Senator Jesse Helms of North Carolina abstained from the measure because it would have allowed the states the option of making abortion legal. He was in favor of an amendment totally banning abortions.

Although it did not pass, the anti-abortionists claimed the vote was a victory for them because they succeeded in getting the HLFA to the floor. The prochoice groups claimed victory because it was defeated. Senator Bob Packwood of Oregon, who lead the opposition to the amendment, said, "We can put it behind us." But that was not the case. The issue has continued to divide Congress.

The Human Life Bills

Because it was so difficult to pass an amendment to the Constitution, the right-to-life legislators tried a different tactic. They introduced "human life" bills instead of amendments. A bill is easier to pass than an amendment. Passage of a bill only requires a majority vote and the signature of the president. Congress can override a presidential veto by a two-thirds vote.

The human life bill, introduced by Senator Jesse Helms in 1981, stated that human life begins at conception and that the Constitution, therefore, protects the fetus and guarantees its rights. Opponents of the bill argued that it interfered with the rights of the woman involved and called the bill unconstitutional. The bill failed to pass.

The following year, Senator Helms introduced a second human life bill. It too said that life begins at conception, but it went a step farther than his earlier bill. It prohibited the use of federal funds for abortions except to save the woman's life. It also prohibited the use of federal funds for abortion research. It too failed.

In the meantime, the Supreme Court had ruled on several cases reaffirming its position that a woman has a right to legal abortion. With President Reagan's backing, the U.S. Justice Department recently asked the Court to repeal the *Roe* v. *Wade* decision and return regulation of abortion to the states. The Justice Department said that the basis for the decision was "flawed."

While the battle over abortion still continues, the anti-abortionists have found other specific ways to restrict the procedure.

Restricting Funds for Abortions

Although the "human life" and states' rights amendments and bills failed to pass in Congress, the anti-abortion groups were victorious in a related area. They managed to have federal funding for abortions cut off. The first funds to be cut were those provided for abortions by Medicaid.

Medicaid provides federal money for medical treatment for low income people and senior citizens. Among the items covered by Medicaid are childbirth and sterilization. The states and the federal government share the costs, and the states administer the money in line with federal guidelines.

For three years after the *Roe* decision, Medicaid routinely covered abortions. Bills banning the use of federal funds for abortions had been introduced in Congress as early as 1974, but they had all been defeated. In 1976, Representative Henry J. Hyde of Illinois introduced a bill in Congress known as the Hyde Amendment. It banned the use of Medicaid funds for abortion.

Congress heatedly debated the Hyde Amendment. Opponents of it saw it as discriminating against poor women who would have to return to illegal abortions, while women with medical insurance or money would be able to obtain legal abortions. Representative Daniel J. Flood of Pennsylvania said, "The Hyde Amendment does not prohibit abortion. It prohibits abortion for poor people. . . . It is a vote against the poor people."

In response, Senator Hyde said, "I would certainly like to prevent, if I could legally, anybody having an abortion, a rich woman, a middle class woman, or a poor woman. Unfortunately, the only vehicle available is the HEW Medicaid bill. A life is a life."

The House of Representatives passed the Hyde Amendment, but the Senate rejected it. For a while, federal funds continued to be used for abortions.

Later that year, a second bill to cut off funds for Medicaid abortions was introduced in Congress. It differed from the first Hyde Amendment because it allowed federal funds to be used for abortions only in cases "where the life of the mother would be clearly endangered" by continuing the pregnancy. Once again, the bill was debated. It clearly made it difficult, if not impossible, for poor women to obtain an abortion, but this time the bill was passed by Congress. It went into effect in 1977.

Those who opposed abortions placed them in the same category as face lifts and hair transplants—medical items that are not necessary. Representative Eldon Rudd of Arizona said, "The cliché we hear most often is, 'A woman has the right to control her own body.' I agree. Let her exercise control—before she gets pregnant. But do not ask the taxpayers of America to pay the price when there is a failure to exercise control by forcing the taxpayers to subsidize the ending of lives of unborn children as a convenience to adult women."

Former President Jimmy Carter, an opponent of abortion, said that the cutting off of funds was unfair. Yet he added, "There are many things in life that are not fair, that wealthy people can afford and poor people can't."

The prochoice supporters countered by saying that almost everyone in the United States is forced to pay taxes for programs they oppose. Pacifists have to pay taxes, a large portion of which goes to the Department of Defense, and Christian Scientists have to pay taxes, a portion of which goes for medical research.

Once the Hyde Amendment was passed, the number of abortions funded by the government dropped from about 295,000 in 1977 to about 2,400 per year. Of the 2,400 abortions, nearly one-third were performed in Ohio, indicating that some states have applied the rules more liberally or strictly than others. The reasons listed in Ohio for the abortions were the following: about 80 percent involved danger to the woman; 17 percent involved severe and long-lasting health damage; 3 percent involved rape or incest.

The prochoice groups challenged the constitutionality of the Hyde Amendment in the courts. There were several class-action suits against it. In the class-action suit *McRae* v. *Matthews,* Judge John F. Dooling of the Second District Court of New York ruled that the Hyde Amendment was unconstitutional. He ruled that it interfered with the First Amendment, which guarantees freedom of religion. His decision was overturned by the Supreme Court. In the light of its decision in favor of abortion in 1973, many people expected the Supreme Court to declare the Hyde Amendment unconstitutional, but it did not do so.

In the *Harris* v. *McRae* (McRae was the Secretary of HEW) ruling, handed down on June 30, 1980, the Supreme Court held that Medicaid was not required to fund "nontherapeutic" or medically unnecessary abortions. Justice Potter Stewart said that it was not up to the Court to decide whether or not the amendment was "wise social policy" but whether or not it was legal. Nevertheless, the Court did define "medically necessary" broadly. It included in its definition the physical, emotional, and psychological health of the woman. Yet, since the ruling, many states have failed to provide Medicaid money, even for those abortions recommended by doctors.

In a related case, *Maher* v. *Roe,* the Court ruled that it is not necessary for a state to provide funds for abortion even though it provides funds for childbirth. The law favoring childbirth, said the Court, did not interfere with a woman's right to seek an abortion using her own funds or private funds. In his dissent, Justice Brennan wrote, "By funding all of the expenses associated with childbirth and none of the expenses in terminating pregnancy, the government literally makes an offer that the indigent woman cannot afford to refuse."

Thus, Congress cut off the Medicaid funds for abortion and the courts supported its action, even though the public was in favor of Medicaid-funded abortions.

According to a 1979 Gallup poll, 70 percent of Americans agreed that Medicaid should pay for abortions for poor women.

In addition to cutting off Medicaid funds, there were other federal budget cuts that restricted abortions. The defense budget barred money for abortions for military personnel or their dependents. The government cut off abortion funds for federal employees—who number close to nine million—and their dependents, and Peace Corps volunteers.

A study done in the late 1970s showed that because of the cutbacks in federal funds, about 5 percent of women eligible for Medicaid carried their unwanted pregnancy to term, and about 1 percent had an illegal abortion. About 94 percent obtained abortion funds from their state or private organizations. The number of late abortions for poor women has risen however, because many of them have trouble finding the money —about $200—quickly.

One woman who resorted to an illegal abortion was Rosie Jimenez. She was the first woman known to have died from an illegal abortion because of the Medicaid cutbacks. She died in 1979. The National Abortion Rights Action League (NARAL) set up a fund in her honor to provide money for abortions for low income women.

The same year, the members of March for Life carried red roses during an anti-abortion demonstration. It was, they said, to remind people of the "beauty of the preborn child." In response, Gloria Steinem, editor of *Ms.,* asked people to send their legislators "one dead rose." The dead rose was to symbolize "the story of

Rosie, a real woman who was once alive, and who died at the age of twenty-seven." Rosie was the first of several women who died from the complications of an illegal abortion in the aftermath of the Hyde Amendment, according to the federal government's Center for Disease Control. The exact number of women who have died in this way is unknown.

Each year, when the federal budget is debated, a new version of the Hyde bill is introduced. Representative William Clay of Missouri has described such anti-abortion tactics as "the Holy Wars all over again." Early versions of the Hyde Amendment allowed government funding of abortions for pregnancies arising from rape or incest. Since 1981, the bills have cut off Medicaid funds for all abortions, unless the woman's pregnancy would endanger her life. President Reagan hailed the new bill and said that rape and incest were used as excuses for abortions; he said only two hundred abortions per year had actually been performed for those reasons.

The various versions of the Hyde Amendment did not require the states to cut off their abortion funding. Even so, by 1979, forty states had moved to restrict Medicaid abortions. Massachusetts was among the states that cut off Medicaid-funded abortions except when the woman's life was in danger. It also eliminated abortion money from state-funded medical insurance for state employees.

Minnesota went a step further. It banned the use of state funds for Planned Parenthood, because the agency offered abortion services as well as birth control. This action was declared illegal by the U.S. District Court of

St. Paul, so the state was forced to provide money for Planned Parenthood's family-planning services.

By 1985, fourteen states and Washington, D.C., provided state funds for abortion. At the same time the anti-abortion groups have been very active in attempting to have the funds cut off. The results of their efforts have been mixed. Colorado, by a slim margin, voted in 1984 to restrict funds for abortions. In Washington, a referendum to prohibit funds for abortions was narrowly defeated in the same year.

As the battle over funding continues, President Reagan has suggested that the federal government should take over the Medicaid program entirely. This would obviously affect thousands of women eligible for Medicaid who want to have an abortion.

Besides cutting off funds within the United States, the anti-abortionists have worked to cut off funds for abortions in foreign countries. In 1984, the United States cut off funds for family-planning organizations operating abroad if the organization offered both birth control and abortion services. For example, the International Planned Parenthood Federation lost $11.5 million in federal funds in 1985 for these reasons. Congress also cut $10 million in federal aid to the United Nations Fund for Population Activities, the largest and most important international organization working on population control. To justify the cut, it said it was responding to reports that women in China are forced to have abortions. The money, in fact, is used in about 140 countries.

Robert L. Schiffer, a former UN official who opposes the cutoff of funds, says that the best way to reduce abortions is through family-planning programs. "[It's] precisely the programs for which the Fund has won recognition and praise."

In addition to cutting off funds, there have been many other ways in which the opponents of abortion have attempted to restrict abortion. Sometimes they have been successful. Sometimes they have failed.

SEVEN

Further Appeal to the Supreme Court

After the Supreme Court's ruling, the prochoice groups became less active. They thought the victory had been won. It was at this time however, that the right-to-life groups really flowered. The strong, single-minded right-to-life movement put the prochoice supporters on the defensive. At the same time all anti-abortionists lobbied nationally to have the *Roe* v. *Wade* decision overturned by Constitutional amendment.

The anti-abortionists, however, found loopholes in *Roe* v. *Wade* and *Doe* v. *Bolton* that enabled them to restrict abortion—at least temporarily. They lobbied for all types of laws to curtail abortion. Some of the laws addressed relatively minor aspects of abortion; others addressed major aspects. Virginia tried to bar advertisements for abortion clinics, Mississippi tried to ban saline abortions. More often than not, the laws were declared unconstitutional, sometimes by the state or federal courts, sometimes when they finally reached the Supreme Court. (To reach the Supreme Court generally took years, as the cases had to work their way through the lower courts.)

There have been several notable Supreme Court cases in which the Court reaffirmed its stand in favor of a woman's right to legal abortion. The Court struck down a number of laws or provisions that interfered with that right. For example, the Pennsylvania Abortion Control Act passed in 1974 made it necessary for a doctor to determine if the fetus was viable or if there was "sufficient reason to believe it may be viable." If so, the doctor was legally bound to use the abortion technique that would provide the "best opportunity for the fetus to be aborted alive." Any doctor who failed to comply with the law was subject to civil and possibly criminal charges. This law was challenged in the case *Collauti* v. *Franklin,* and was struck down by a three-judge federal panel in 1977. The case was taken on appeal to the Supreme Court, where the lower court decision was upheld. The Supreme Court based its decision on the fact that the definition of viability was not clear and that "different physicians equate viability with different probabilities of survival, and some physicians refuse to equate viability with any numerical probability at all." It also said that normal medical care did not cover such occurrences and that the law could have a "profound chilling effect on physicians." Only Justice Byron R. White dissented. He felt that the state had the power to protect a viable fetus and that doing so was not in violation of the *Roe* decision.

In 1976, the state of Missouri passed a restrictive abortion law that used a different tactic. The law required a woman seeking an abortion to have the written consent of her husband or of her parents if she was a minor. It also required the patient to sign an "informed consent" statement. It required doctors to keep records on abortion and to try to save the aborted fetus just as they would try to save a premature infant. It was challenged in the courts in the case *Danforth* v. *Planned Parenthood of Central Missouri,* and like many of the others went all the way up to the Supreme Court.

In July 1976, the Supreme Court ruled six to three against Missouri. It said that a woman does not need her husband's consent in order to have an abortion. It was decided that since the state cannot veto a woman's abortion because it is her right, then her husband cannot veto it on the same grounds. The majority stated, "It is difficult to believe that the goal of fostering mutuality and trust in a marriage and of strengthening the marital relationship and the marriage institution, will be achieved by giving the husband a veto power exercisable for any reason whatsoever or for no reason at all."

In the *Danforth* case, the Court also ruled that the right to privacy of a woman who is underage is more important than a parent's right to veto an abortion. The antichoice groups argued that all medical procedures for minors, even getting their ears pierced, required parental permission. The Court, however, said abortion was different. It is the woman, said the Court, that is most affected by the pregnancy, not the family, so it is up to her to decide whether to have an abortion or not.

In the same decision, the Supreme Court upheld two provisions of the Missouri law. It ruled that the state was allowed to require a written "informed consent" statement from the woman in advance of an abortion. It also allowed the state to require doctors to keep records on abortion. The Court struck down the very important provision requiring doctors to try to save the life of the fetus.

Later, Missouri passed a law that made it mandatory for doctors to tell patients that if the fetus was aborted alive it would become a ward of the state. The law was declared unconstitutional by the state supreme court— a decision that was endorsed by the Supreme Court in 1979.

Despite the Court's ruling in *Danforth,* several states, such as Massachusetts, continued trying to restrict abortions for minors by requiring parental permission. Under the Massachusetts law, the parents of the minor, or a judge, had to give approval before a minor could have an abortion. The law was challenged and went on to the Supreme Court. In the case *Bellotti* v. *Baird,* the Court declared the law unconstitutional and said it placed an "undue burden" on the minor. In a later decision, *H. L.* v. *Matheson,* the Supreme Court modified its decision in *Bellotti* v. *Baird.* It ruled that states can require a doctor to notify parents of an "immature" minor before performing an abortion. Again the Court stated that the parents of "mature" minors need not be notified or give their approval.

A well-known case concerned the law passed in Akron, Ohio, in 1979 that required doctors to obtain "informed consent" before performing an abortion.

"Informed consent" included a description of the fetus at every week of its development. The law also called for a twenty-four-hour waiting period before the abortion could be performed and for all abortions after the first trimester to be done in a hospital.

Naturally, choice supporters challenged the legality of the Akron law, in the case *City of Akron* v. *Akron Center for Reproductive Health*. It took a year and a half for the Federal District Court for the Northern District of Ohio to rule on the law. Eventually the law was declared unconstitutional apart from the provision requiring a twenty-four-hour waiting period. The case was appealed and went to the Supreme Court.

Finally, in 1983, the Supreme Court, by a six to three decision, struck down the entire Akron law. That same year it also ruled against laws requiring that second trimester abortions be done in a hospital and against other restrictive measures. The Akron decision has been viewed as a landmark, precedent-setting case, however, and several federal courts have used it as a basis for their decisions.

Justices Rehnquist, White, and O'Connor dissented in the Akron decision. O'Connor said, "Recent studies have demonstrated increasingly earlier fetal viability. It is certainly reasonable to believe that fetal viability in the first trimester of pregnancy may be possible in the not-too-distant future. The *Roe* framework is clearly on a collision with itself." In other words, she believes that medical technology will eventually negate the *Roe* decision and make abortion subject to state regulation. The Supreme Court had given the states the right to regulate abortion once the fetus is considered viable.

Before the Akron decision was made, Pennsylvania again attempted to pass legislation to restrict abortion with the Abortion Control Act of 1982. This law required parental consent for a minor's abortion and the doctor to inform a patient of the "detrimental" effects of abortion. In 1984, a federal circuit court declared these sections of the law unconstitutional. The decisions were based on the precedents established by the Supreme Court. But the state appealed the case to the upper court, which accepted it for review in 1985. The Court's action is unusual, given the previous *Akron* decision.

In 1985, the Supreme Court made a second unusual decision. It agreed to hear the appeal for a case challenging the Illinois Abortion Law which was passed in 1975, even though the law has since been changed. It is very rare for the Supreme Court to rule on laws that are no longer in effect. The Illinois Abortion Law, as passed initially, made it a crime for a doctor to cause the death of a viable fetus by performing an abortion. It also required doctors to inform patients that birth control methods such as IUDs induce abortion. The state court declared those sections of the law unconstitutional, so the law was amended. Nevertheless, the case was appealed to the upper court.

Because the Court's action was so unusual, the choice advocates saw it as a threat to legal abortion, particularly because the then Chief Justice Warren Burger voted in favor of reviewing the Illinois and Pennsylvania laws. He had previously voted in favor of legal abortion in *Roe* and had voted to reaffirm *Roe* in cases such as

Akron. The choice advocates were worried that Burger would change his opinion on abortion, and he did. He was among the dissenting justices when the Supreme Court struck down Pennsylvania law in a five to four decision on June 11, 1986 in the case *Thornburgh* v. *American College of Obstetricians and Gynecologists.* The Court ruled against the 1982 Pennsylvania law on the grounds that sections of the law were designed to deter women from having abortions and that it required doctors to risk the health of the woman for the sake of late term fetuses. Justice Blackmun said, "The states are not free, under the guise of protecting maternal health or potential life, to intimidate women into continuing pregnancies."

The four minority opinions in the case were seen as very strong. In his dissent Justice White said that because abortion is a "hotly contested moral and political issue" it should be decided by the "will of the people." Thus, he believed it was proper to overturn *Roe.*

Burger only went so far as to state, ". . . we should re-examine *Roe.*" It was not the intent of the Court, he noted, to allow abortion on demand. He emphasized the states' right to regulate abortion to protect the health of the woman as well as the "potentiality of human life." In his opinion, the Court had ignored the limitations on abortion established by *Roe.*

When it was made, the *Roe* decision was seven to two in favor of legalized abortion. Therefore the narrow vote upholding *Roe* in this case was viewed as a significant threat to legal abortion. Douglas Johnson, Director of the National Right-to-Life Committee, said, "We're very encouraged. . . . We're just one vote away from a Court which may be prepared to abandon *Roe* v. *Wade.*"

The Supreme Court can change its position on abortion. It can review, revise, or reverse previous decisions. This is likely to happen as new justices are appointed to the Court, if they are anti-abortion. In 1981, Justice Sandra Day O'Connor, an anti-abortionist, was appointed to the Supreme Court. She was the youngest justice on the bench at the time. In the cases that have come before the court since her nomination, she has voted in favor of restrictive abortion laws passed by the states.

At the beginning of 1986 four justices, all prochoice, were over the age of seventy-five. Each time one or more retires or dies, President Reagan has the opportunity to replace them with justices who would take positions against abortion.

In mid 1986 just such a significant event took place. Chief Justice Warren Burger resigned from the Supreme Court and Justice William H. Rehnquist, an opponent of legal abortion, was appointed Chief Justice. Antonin Scalia, also an opponent of abortion, was appointed to fill Rehnquist's place on the bench. The prochoice groups were dismayed by these appointments. In its first abortion case however, the Rehnquist court forbade Arizona to cut off funds for Planned Parenthood. In effect, the five to three ruling makes it impossible for any state to stop funds for private groups which provide abortions or abortion counseling. Planned Parenthood had challenged the law in Arizona on the grounds that it violated the right of free speech. The Court concurred with this view.

The Supreme Court may change its position on abortion in the future. The possible reversal of the *Roe* decision is the greatest threat to legal abortion.

If the Supreme Court changes its position, the anti-abortionists will be ready. Idaho, for example, has passed a law requiring the governor to ban abortion if the Court makes it possible.

Meanwhile, the anti-abortionists have found more colorful ways to protest abortion. Every anniversary of the *Roe* decision, March for Life organizes a parade up Pennsylvania Avenue in Washington, D.C., to the Supreme Court building, where the demonstrators stop. They usually carry signs reading "Thank God, Jesus Wasn't Aborted" and "Abortion Is Murder." Estimates of the size of the crowds have ranged from 20,000 to 60,000 marchers.

EIGHT

The Right-to-Life Movement and Protest

At a local level, the anti-abortionists have tried to restrict abortion by lobbying for zoning laws which ban abortion clinics. It took three years for such a zoning law, passed in 1975 in Southboro, Massachusetts, to reach the state supreme court. It was then declared illegal.

Elsewhere, towns have attempted to pass regulations governing abortion clinics that are so stringent that it becomes difficult, if not impossible, for the clinics to operate. Often such laws are overturned, but at the very least they cause delays and cost the plaintiffs, that is the party complaining, a great deal in legal fees. When Susan Hill requested a business permit to open an abortion clinic in Fairfield, New Jersey, the permit was refused. She went to court and it cost her $300,000 in legal expenses and took four years to fight the case.

When anti-abortionists have failed to ban clinics they have found ways to harass them. They use methods such as tying up the phones at clinics. As a member of the group Women Exploited by Abortion says, "A lot of people call it harassment, but I call it education."

The right-to-life groups have been known to set up counseling centers with names that make them sound like abortion clinics. When a woman goes into one of these centers, people attempt to talk her out of having an abortion. Said NOW vice president Mary Jean Collins, "The tactics of misleading advertising and harassment are especially traumatic to young women."

The National Right to Life Committee officially endorsed sit-ins and picketing in 1978, saying, "Abortion represents the epitome of violence to our unborn."

At abortion clinics all over the country, picketers show up on the doorsteps as soon as the clinic opens. The demonstrators hand out anti-abortion literature and carry photographs of well-developed fetuses, which look like babies. Such photographs have a strong emotional impact on women. Thanks to advances in photography, it is possible to photograph the fetus in the womb. Recently, *Life* magazine published an astounding picture story of the development of the fetus. This generated a great deal of response. Science writer Albert Rosenfeld says, "[many woman] wrote in to say that they could never again think of their *babies as disposable things*" (his italics).

At other clinics, right-to-life supporters sometimes sing songs such as "Where Have All the Children Gone?" They sometimes shout "murderer" and "killer" at the doctors and patients. They fill up garbage cans with dolls splattered in red paint. They show photographs of bloody, aborted fetuses to the women who arrive and say to them, "Please don't kill your baby."

The demonstrations at the clinics are legal, provided the patients are not intimidated or coerced. The First Amendment guarantees freedom of speech and peaceful assembly. The courts, however, have set limits on the demonstrations to protect the privacy of the patients. For example, they have limited the number of protesters who can assemble, the times at which protests may be made, and the types of signs the protestors can carry. They have restrained anti-abortionists from taking photographs of a woman entering a clinic, and then calling the woman's family, co-workers, or friends to tell them that she has had an abortion.

The protesters occasionally make such a nuisance of themselves that the police are called, and they are arrested for trespassing. Being arrested can make them feel noble, and they have been known to compare themselves to civil rights leaders like Martin Luther King, Jr.

Joseph M. Scheidler, founder of the Pro-Life Action League and author of *CLOSED: 99 Ways to Stop Abortion*, calls nonpicketers "wimps for life." He is proud of the fact that he has been arrested five times and brags that his tactics have resulted in the closing of eighteen abortion clinics.

Although the NRLC condemned violence at the clinics, in the 1980s the demonstrations began to grow uglier. Several of the more radical antichoice demonstrators started to force their way into clinics. On one occasion at the Delaware Women's Health Organization, they barged into the clinic. Before the police could get there, they had torn wrappers off sterilized medical supplies and had hidden parts of the suction machines used for the abortions.

The tactics of some of the protesters are sometimes even more extreme. Reverend Norman Stone stood outside a clinic in Appleton, Wisconsin, holding an aborted fetus. He held it up to show it to the women entering the clinic. He called the fetus Baby Ray. He was convicted of trespassing, but not of carrying a corpse. The district attorney noted that it is illegal to walk around the city with a corpse, "but this is not a corpse because it has never been born." Of course, if the court had ruled that the fetus were a corpse, it would have supported the right-to-life position that abortion is murder. This action put the choice supporters in a difficult spot.

In Forest Grove, Oregon, Catholics United for Life were among the groups to show up outside a clinic with a twenty-week-old fetus. They showed it to first-graders walking by. The *New York Times* quoted Dr. Peter Bours, who heads the clinic, as recalling, "[They] said, 'This is a baby and the doctor in there is killing them for $1,000 a baby.'" (The doctor's fee is $140 for an abortion.)

Even so, the worst was yet to come. Dr. Bours was the target of angry letters to the local newspaper. Then his clinic was firebombed and his life was threatened. He was told that his head would be cut off and left in a public place where his enemies could urinate on it.

As a result of the anti-abortion protests, Dr. Bours medical practice dropped off. The number of deliveries he was asked to perform dropped from about 300 to about 150 per year. In the *New York Times* he said that about half of the people stopped coming to him because they oppose abortion and the other half are "simply worried that someone was going to try to blow the place up while they were in there." Finally, Dr. Bours changed his practice and stopped delivering babies. What happened to him was not an isolated event. It was the start of a new and dangerous trend.

The Turn Toward Violence

Only a handful of anti-abortionists endorse threats or violence against doctors and clinics performing abortions. The overwhelming majority of prolifers oppose terrorist tactics. Many do feel, however, that they should take advantage of the exposure. The violence has given the right-to-life movement increased coverage by the media. In fact, the exposure may have lead to even more violence.

The National Abortion Federation (NAF) represents over 300 clinics, hospitals, and doctors' offices. None of its members received bomb threats before 1977, but with each succeeding year after that, the number of threats increased. In 1984, fifty-one of the NAF's members received threats of violence and at least eighteen clinic directors were threatened with death. One was kidnapped and held for eight days.

Many acts of violence were carried out. Bombs exploded in twenty-five abortion or family-planning clinics throughout the United States, including those in Mesquite, Texas; Columbus, Ohio; San Diego, Pomona, and Santa Ana, California; Fayetteville, Arkansas; and

Granite City, Illinois. There were several physical attacks on clinic workers. Two men bombed two clinics and a doctor's office in Pensacola, Florida, at Christmas. They described their actions as a "gift to Jesus on his birthday."

In April 1985, Joseph M. Scheidler organized a gathering to plan protests. Thirty-four protesters met in Appleton, Wisconsin, to plan a "year of pain and fear" for clinics and hospitals.

Winston Wilder, president of the Dallas Abortion Abolition Society, was quoted in the press as saying, "It's time to get mean." He feels that making it difficult for a woman to enter a clinic will help prevent abortions. He often stands outside the abortion clinics in Dallas and takes pictures of the women entering them.

In defending the bombings and terroristlike tactics, Paul Brown, head of the American Life League, said that the members of his group answer not to the law of the country but to a "higher law," or God's law. He added, "[The bombers] never hurt anybody. They may have destroyed a building or two, but they have not done anything to hurt a person." In fact, it has been luck that people have not been hurt so far. A package sent to the Feminist Women's Health Center in Portland, Oregon, was designed to explode when opened. Because it looked suspicious, the police were called, and the post office tracked down a similar package addressed to the Planned Parenthood Center. On December 10, 1985, a bomb went off in the bathroom of a New York City clinic during the day. If anyone had been in the bathroom, it is very likely that he or she would have been killed.

Bill Baird operates an abortion clinic in Hempstead, New York, and he said in January 1986, "I've never seen this much violence go unchallenged." He had to put his family into hiding, and every day he has to check his car and mail for bombs.

Both Reverend Jerry Falwell and Ronald Reagan were lambasted for remaining silent for so long about the terrorist tactics. Finally, as the violence got worse and worse, they condemned it. Falwell said, the violence "sets us back to the Stone Age."

The protests and the violence have greatly affected the operation of some clinics. They have had to become almost armed fortresses. They have had to install bullet-proof windows. They have asked volunteers to escort patients to their cars. They have played religious music to annoy the protesters and drown out the shouts. Groups such as NOW and Planned Parenthood have set up vigils to protect the clinics against violence. Because of the violence, insurance companies have either refused to insure some clinics or have raised their rates enormously. In addition, many doctors have refused to perform abortions in clinics.

The choice advocates often complain that the police fail to enforce the law when anti-abortionists storm a clinic. There are reports that the police are reluctant to step into such a heated controversy. Of course, the protesters often stop their illegal actions before the police arrive. According to Susan Hill, executive director of the Women's Health Organization, patients are also reluctant to press charges. They do not want to testify in court that on their way to have an abortion they were harassed or shoved.

In response to the terrorist tactics, former NOW president Judy Goldsmith said, "We have blocked the anti-abortion fanatics before, and we will do it again. We will not allow them to make abortion illegal or impossible. We are as determined to block them in the streets as in the legislatures and the courts."

When a clinic is at the center of protest, it affects the physical and mental health of the patient. Research by the National Abortion Federation revealed that the rate of complications is four times higher at such clinics. There are more blood clots, higher pulse rates, more intense cramps, and more fevers. There are also more instances of sloppy abortion practices, such as leaving fetal tissue in the body, which may mean the woman requires a second abortion. The protests also frighten women off so they put off going for the abortion. The number of abortions performed during the second trimester is also up.

Although the vast majority of anti-abortionists oppose the terrorists tactics, they are glad that the violence has given their case additional media coverage. The networks, said a sociologist, are "obsessed" with getting both sides of the story, especially because it's explosive and because the newscasters are biased in favor of abortion. In fact, say many, the networks go out of their way to air the anti-abortion view, even when it verges on propaganda.

Molding Public Opinion

The anti-abortion groups, like the prochoice groups, attempt to mold public opinion in many ways. One of their most successful efforts was the production and distribution of the anti-abortion film "The Silent Scream." It was produced by American Portrait Films, whose president is a member of the organization Crusade for Life.

"The Silent Scream" shows an abortion of a twelve-week-old fetus through the use of ultrasonic pictures. Dr. Bernard N. Nathanson narrates the film, and he says that the fetus shown is feeling pain and issuing a "silent scream."

The prochoice groups describe the film as propaganda. The American College of Obstetricians and Gynecologists issued a statement saying there is no scientific evidence that a fetus feels pain in the first trimester. They also contend that the fetus's lungs are not fully developed; therefore, it cannot scream.

In a rebuttal videotape, "A Planned Parenthood Response to The Silent Scream," a panel of doctors dispute the narration of "The Silent Scream." They say that a twelve-week-old fetus cannot feel pain, since its brain and nervous system are not developed.

"The Silent Scream" received wide publicity when it was released for distribution. It was aired in part or in its entirety by scores of TV stations, including the networks. Sometimes the television station attempted to balance the news report. On the *CBS Morning News*, Dr. Jennifer Niebyl of the Johns Hopkins School of Medicine disputed the claims made by the film. She noted that Dr. Nathanson says the fetus is fighting the abortion. She pointed out that the film techniques used distort the movement of the fetus. Even so, to many viewers the fetus does look like a baby moving, and they find watching the film emotionally wrenching.

Former NOW president Judy Goldsmith said, "Many of us remember the undeniable fact that, in the days before abortion was made safe and legal, women's screams were not silent."

Copies of "The Silent Scream" were sent to the members of Congress and thousands of state legislators and judges. It was shown at the White House, and President Ronald Reagan endorsed it. He said, "If every member of Congress could see it, they would move quickly to end the tragedy of abortion." It was also shown in churches, on college campuses, and even in high schools.

"The Silent Scream" was translated into ten languages and distributed worldwide. Over 15,000 copies of it were distributed and the antichoice groups made it their goal to distribute it to every church in the country.

The controversy over "The Silent Scream" gave it a high degree of publicity. Such tactics seem to put the prochoice groups on the defensive. Yet there has been no change in public attitudes regarding abortion—a majority still supports legal abortion.

The Prochoice Response

For a while, the prochoice groups didn't do much. Once abortion was legalized, they thought the battle was over, so the strength and fervor of the right-to-life movement caught them temporarily off guard. Then they began to mobilize again.

The *NOW York Woman,* the newsletter of the National Organization for Women, New York City chapter, recently warned, "It can happen—women can lose the right to make choices about their reproductive lives if we don't stand up for our rights now."

✱The right to an abortion was a key issue at the 1985 NOW convention. Judy Goldsmith said, "We must establish, once and for all, that reproductive freedom is as fundamental a right as life, liberty, and the pursuit of happiness." In response, the delegates chanted, "We will not go back." Outside the convention hall, members of the Louisiana Right to Life Federation picketed and carried signs reading SAVE THE BABY and ABORTION IS MURDER.

A NOW campaign was started to obtain signatures of at least a million people who support legal abortion. At about the same time, the National Abortion Rights Action League launched its own campaign called "Silent No More." It asked women to admit that they had had an abortion and to speak out about the reasons leading to it. Over 40,000 women, including many celebrities, wrote letters.

Gloria Steinem, editor of *Ms.* magazine, said that "if a woman sits with her family or friends, she will find people who have had abortions and who will be supportive of her." She herself was among those who admitted to having had an illegal abortion.

It is not easy for a woman to admit to having had an abortion. So many feel ashamed of it because of the pressure by the right-to-life groups. Others are afraid to alienate friends or co-workers who are against abortion. In 1985, *People* magazine asked 109 well-known women if they support legal abortion. Only twenty-eight agreed to have their answers printed. Six said no. The six were

Joanne Kemp, wife of Senator Jack Kemp, who opposes abortion; Senator Paula Hawkins; Clare Boothe Luce, playwright and former Congresswoman; Marabel Morgan, author of the traditionalist book *The Total Woman;* Phyllis Schlafly, who led the fight against the Equal Rights Amendment; and Faith Whittlesey, former ambassador and lawyer.

Often the women who vividly described their illegal abortions did so anonymously. They talked about the dirty conditions, the pain due to lack of anesthesia, the shame and guilt, the breakup of their relationships, the "grinding," "snipping" noises, and the squirting of blood and fluids.

NOW organized a dramatic appeal for the continuation of legal abortion in 1986 when it sent hangers to anti-abortion legislators. On the hangers were tags that read, "You make the choice for all women—safe, legal abortion or this."

Like the right-to-lifers, the prochoice groups organized their own marches and protests. A mass demonstration was held in Washington, D.C., on March 9, 1986. Susan Dworkin, a contributing editor to *Ms.,* said that she expected to see about 10,000 demonstrators. About 100,000 showed up. The prochoice groups are as determined to keep abortion legal as the antichoice groups are to ban it.

NINE

Abortion in
the Past

Abortion is not new. It has been practiced since the beginning of civilization and has always been opposed by some and accepted by others. Throughout history, a wide variety of methods, many extremely painful, have been used to bring about an abortion. Women have inserted pastes made of mashed ants and gunpowder into their wombs; they have poured boiling water on their bellies or have beaten their bellies with stones; they have climbed trees or have exercised vigorously. Many of the methods have not worked but caused damage and even death to the woman.

About five thousand years ago in China, women would drink quicksilver or swallow fourteen live tadpoles to try to bring on their menstrual period. In ancient Egypt, women would attempt to abort themselves by inserting paste and crocodile dung into their uteri.

In the course of civilization, abortion laws have varied greatly. In ancient Assyria, abortion was a crime. Women who had an abortion were put on trial, and if convicted, they were impaled on a stake and given no burial.

Babylonian laws, known as the Code of Hammurabi (about 1750 B.C.), did not make abortion a crime, although causing a pregnant woman to miscarry was a criminal offense. The same was true of Jewish law.

Abortion was practiced in the ancient city-states of Greece. The Greeks used both surgery and drugs for abortions. It was against the law only if the husband was not told about it, or if the woman died as a result. The great philosophers Aristotle and Plato advocated abortion as a way to control the population. Aristotle, however, was only in favor of abortion before there is "sensation and life."

Hippocrates, famous for inspiring the Hippocratic Oath (about 400 B.C.), which doctors still take, was against abortion. On the other hand, Soranos of Ephesus, the well-known doctor, approved of abortion for three reasons: to conceal adultery, to maintain feminine beauty, and to avoid danger to the mother.

In Rome, abortion was legal because the fetus was thought of as part of the woman. A woman's husband had the right to demand that she have an abortion, and he had the right to punish or divorce her if she had one without his permission.

Historically, religious teachings on abortion have not been clear. Neither the Talmud nor the Bible talk about induced abortions. The book of Exodus (chapter 21 verses 22–23) in the Bible is often cited as evidence that abortion is wrong, but the passage is really about accidental miscarriage. It says that a miscarriage as a result of violence is a capital offense. Many early Christian theologians, however, taught that abortion is wrong.

The early Christian book *The Teaching of the Twelve Apostles* says, "You shall not slay a child by abortion. You shall not kill what has been generated." Likewise, the *Epistle of Barnabas* (c. 138) was against abortion. Later Christians condemned abortion even more. Some historians say this was a result of their opposition to pagan Roman attitudes and morals.

By the fourth century, the Catholic Church required a ten-year penance for women who had abortions—a less severe penance than that required for homicide, which lasted for life.

During the next century, a split developed between the Eastern Catholic Church and the Western Catholic Church. The Eastern theologians condemned abortion. But many Western Christian theologians were not against early abortions. In defense of abortion, they quoted St. Augustine, who believed, "There cannot yet be said to be a soul in a body that lacks sensation." According to St. Augustine, a male fetus was ensouled at forty days and a female at eighty days. Interestingly, there was no scientific method for determining the sex of the fetus!

The word used to describe the sensation of fetal movement was *quickening.* Quickening generally occurs between the fourth and sixth months. For centuries, quickening was the only way for the woman to be sure she was pregnant, because there were no medical tests to confirm pregnancies.

Between the fifth and twelfth centuries, several Church councils condemned abortion, yet the concept of a "formed" or "unformed" fetus had taken hold. The *Decretum,* a book on ecclesiastic law written about 1140 by the Italian canonist Gratian, accepted abortion. It said, "He is not a murderer who brings about abortion before the soul is in the body."

Throughout the Middle Ages and the Renaissance in Europe, abortion was legal until quickening occurred. *The Canon of Medicine,* a medical text, listed several ways to induce abortions: exercise, lifting heavy objects, drugs, baths, and jumping.

Within the Catholic Church between 1450 and 1750 there were conflicting opinions regarding abortion. In 1588, Pope Sixtus V stated that abortion was the same as homicide and subject to the same penalties. Only three years later, Pope Gregory XVI eliminated those penalties until after the fetus was ensouled—forty days after conception.

Eventually, the theory of the forty- and eighty-day ensoulment process lost credibility because of advances in biology, particularly the discovery of the egg and sperm. Theologians then became convinced that ensoulment was more likely to occur at conception than forty days later. In 1869, Pope Pius IX changed Church law and made the penalty for abortion excommunication regardless of the stage of development of the fetus. At about the same time abortion was banned in most of Europe.

In his 1930 encyclical on marriage, Pope Pius XI called abortion a "very serious crime." He wrote,

> The lives of both [the woman and the fetus] are equally sacred and no one, not even public authority, can ever have the right to destroy them. It is absurd to invoke against innocent human beings the right of the State to inflict capital punishment, for this is valid only against the guilty. Nor is there any question here of the right of self-defense, even to the shedding of blood, against an unjust assailant, for none could describe as an unjust assailant an innocent child. Nor, finally, does there exist any so-called right of extreme necessity which could extend to the direct killing of an innocent human being.

According to Pope Pius XI, the only acceptable abortion was an indirect abortion, for example, the removal of the fetus in an ectopic pregnancy or to cure uterine cancer.

Pope Pius XII often spoke about abortion. He said, "Even the unborn child is a human being in the same degree and by the same title as its mother." His successor, Pope John XXIII, also viewed conception as the beginning of life and said, "Directly willed and procured abortion, even if for therapeutic reasons, are to be absolutely excluded as licit means of regulating birth."

The present position of the Roman Catholic Church is that abortion takes a human life and is therefore wrong. At the same time, there are Catholic philosophers such as Bernard Haring who do not share the official view of abortion. Although he is personally opposed to abortion except in rare circumstances, he says, "The theory of successive ensoulment of the embryo . . . is gaining ground once more."

America's abortion policies were patterned on those of Great Britain, which had no laws on abortion until the thirteenth century. At that time, abortions performed after quickening were made illegal, but the penalties were not as harsh as those for murder. The laws were based on the Christian teaching that the fetus was "ensouled" at the time of quickening. It was not until the 1800s that all abortions were made illegal in Britain.

In the New World colonies, it is estimated that one out of every five or six pregnancies performed in the 1700s ended in abortion. Those who had abortions were mostly single women in the middle and upper classes.

In 1803, abortion was made illegal in England both before and after quickening, but the penalties were less severe for abortions done before quickening. In the United States, however, the laws were not changed and abortion continued to be legal.

Abortions were legal in the United States before quickening right up until the middle of the 1800s. In 1809, the Massachusetts State Supreme Court dismissed an indictment for abortion because no one was able to prove the woman was "quick with child." In 1812, in the *Commonwealth* v. *Bangs* decision, the same court again ruled that abortion before quickening was not against the law.

Throughout the 1800s, there were many advertisements, even in family newspapers and the religious press, for do-it-yourself methods of inducing abortion. The techniques included bloodletting, hot baths, douching, jumping off chairs, and electric shocks. Drugs such as oil of tansy were used. None of these methods were very effective and some, being mild poisons, were actually dangerous. There were advertisements for what were called "Portuguese Female Pills." They were abortifacients (abortion inducers), and they were advertised as a cure for "menstrual obstruction," a euphemism for pregnancy. The Sir James Clarke's Celebrated Female Pills carried the warning: "These pills should not be taken by females that are pregnant, during the FIRST THREE MONTHS, as they are sure to bring on MISCARRIAGE. . . ." The warning, of course, was actually bringing women the message they wanted.

Connecticut was the first state to pass laws governing abortion. The state made it a crime in 1821 to give a woman "quick with child" a poison intended to make her miscarry. Actually, the law was aimed more at controlling the use of poisons than at controlling abortion. It was amended in 1830 to ban all methods of abortion after quickening.

In 1830, New York made it a crime to perform abortions after quickening. "Therapeutic abortions" or those necessary to save the life of the woman were exempted, however. This was the first law that gave doctors the right to make the abortion decision. In 1845, New York was also the first state to make the woman subject to prosecution for having an abortion.

The more stringent abortion laws had little, if any, effect. Abortionists like Madame Restell of New York made fortunes, charging as much as $300! The practice of abortion continued to be so widespread that the *New York Times* condemned it in a long article on August 23, 1871. Doctors said that as many as 50 percent of all pregnancies ended before birth, most by intent.

The openness of abortion was one reason why the states began to try to control it. Between 1821 and 1841, ten states and one territory passed laws that made abortion after quickening a crime unless the woman's life was at stake. It is important to note that during the 1800s and continuing well into the 1900s, there were many diseases or medical conditions that were considered dangerous for a pregnant woman. These included heart disease, tuberculosis, and continual vomiting as well as the problems associated with pregnancy, such as toxemia, which is poisoning of the blood.

The rest of the states soon followed suit in making abortions after quickening illegal, but the penalties were light and the laws all but ignored. For example, Massachusetts made performing an abortion a misdemeanor unless the woman died. In any case, the abortionists were rarely prosecuted and even more rarely convicted. When convicted, the abortionists were often only put on probation.

The anti-abortion movement was really spurred on by the American Medical Association. Founded in 1847, the AMA was established to upgrade the status of the profession. At the time doctors were not respected or well paid. They were also in competition with folk healers and abortionists. Medical procedures such as bleeding and harsh laxatives were commonly used by doctors, while folk healers often used milder home treatments like herbs and baths. The doctors wanted to set themselves apart from folk healers and abortionists, so they lobbied to establish licensing. In 1854, the *Boston Medical and Surgical Journal* said abortion must be very common, judging by the "great number of half-grown infants found floating in boxes upon the water and dropped in vaults. . . ."

In 1859, at the urging of Dr. Horatio Storer, an abortion expert and opponent, the AMA passed a resolution condemning abortion. Its members were asked to write anti-abortion articles and books. Many of them said that scientific evidence proved that human life began at conception. Actually, what science had discovered was that the egg and sperm unite before the fetus develops. In *Roe* v. *Wade,* the Supreme Court noted that the doctors' attitudes in the late 1800s "may have played a significant role in the enactment of stringent criminal abortion legislation during that period. . . ."

Doctors condemned abortion, but not the women having abortions. They said that the women were ignorant of the medical facts. This gave doctors a claim to medical knowledge that the folk healers lacked. They also highly publicized the problems abortions caused and the possible infections. There were no antibiotics or antiseptics, so many women did die as a result of an abortion. Of course, many other women died giving birth.

Despite the AMA's stand on the issue, abortion continued to flourish. The *Detroit Review of Medicine and Pharmacy* at that time said, "Among married persons so extensive has this practice become, that people of high repute not only commit this crime, but do not even shun to speak [of it]. . . ."

When the Civil War began in 1860, abortion before quickening was still legal in all but three states. After the Civil War, however, state after state revised their laws to make abortions illegal. This was not a result of a grass roots movement against abortion; in many cases, the laws were designed to protect the woman, not the fetus. A court in New Jersey said, "The statute regards her as the victim of the crime, not as the criminal."

By 1880, over forty states or territories made abortion a crime whenever it was performed during the pregnancy. For example, abortion was declared "assault with intent to murder" in Georgia in 1876. There were exemptions for therapeutic abortions in all but six of the state laws. As noted earlier, a wide variety of complaints were taken into account for a therapeutic abortion.

Abortion became a national issue in 1872, when Congress passed the Comstock Act. This act prohibited the use of the mail to sell, lend, or give away "obscene material." "Obscene materials" included birth control or abortion drugs or devices. Birth control devices were sold in pornography shops at the time. This was the Victorian era, when sex for pleasure was considered "bad," and when many doctors warned that sex could be physically destructive.

The Comstock Act was in effect until the 1930s, and the anti-abortion stance of the states continued too. Yet, the birth rate in the United States declined from 1800 to 1900. In 1800, the average number of children born to a woman was seven. By the next century, the number was down to 3.5. Since many of the most effective methods of birth control, such as the pill and the IUD, were not available, it is clear that abortion was practiced regularly—either under the guise of "medically necessary" abortions, or underground. Probably a high percentage of abortions were performed by midwives or by older women who passed on their knowledge to younger women. There are estimates that as many as two million abortions a year took place in the 1890s, and that between 1850 and 1900 one out of every five or six pregnancies ended in abortion.

In 1896, a doctor wrote that "Good and exemplary women, who would rather part with their right hands or let their tongues cleave to the roof of the mouth than to commit a crime, seem to believe that prior to quickening it is no more harm to cause the evacuation of the contents of their wombs than it is that of their bladders or their bowels." This attitude continued for a very long time.

In his book *Abortion,* written in 1936, Frederick Taussig noted, "We are amazed at the frankness with which decent women speak about [abortion] among themselves and with their physician. . . . It is without any feeling of guilt. . . . The most striking evidence of the attitude of the public is the fact that, even when positive evidence of guilt is brought in the trial of an abortionist, he is rarely punished by the jury." In Alabama, between 1894 and 1932 there were forty indictments brought against abortionists and only five convictions. In the 1940s Alfred Kinsey, famous for his study on sexual behavior, *The Kinsey Report,* asked women if they had had an abortion. About 22 percent of the married women answered yes.

Not all of the abortions were illegal. All the states allowed abortions to save the life of the woman, so many doctors took a woman's overall health and mental health into consideration and performed the operation, even if the pregnancy would not literally "kill" the woman. Doctors argued amongst themselves on when an abortion was acceptable, but very few people, including the doctors, were troubled by these disagreements. Until the late 1940s, medical problems such as heart irregularities, polio, stomach and intestinal diseases, arthritis, diabetes, and tuberculosis were still grounds for a woman to have an abortion.

When medical advances made pregnancy less and less dangerous, it became more difficult for doctors to perform abortions on the grounds that the pregnancy was dangerous to the woman. Doctors began to lose control over abortion. By the 1950s, many hospitals had established boards of doctors who had to approve the abortion.

Abortion moved out of the realm of medical issues into the realm of moral and political issues. Then the pendulum began to swing again and the movement to liberalize or reform the abortion laws took root. Among those who were in the forefront of it were doctors.

TEN

Abortion Around the World

Abortion is a worldwide practice, regardless of whether it is legal or not. The global trend is toward liberal policies. The movement to make abortion legal took place not only in the United States, but in many countries around the world. In some places it happened sooner, in others later. In some countries, such as the Soviet Union, the laws have fluctuated between being restrictive and liberal. It is estimated that worldwide there is one abortion for every five births, or about 55 million abortions per year.

In 1971, about 38 percent of the world's population lived in countries where abortion was legal. By the end of the decade this figure had jumped to 67 percent. The World Health Organization estimated that in 1976 about 50 million abortions occurred in the world; more than half of them—35 million—were legal.

Although legal abortion is spreading, illegal abortions are not uncommon in places where laws are restrictive, such as Latin America, the Middle East, and Africa. Worldwide as many as 86,000 women die every year as a result of complications from illegal abortion, the number-one cause of death among women of childbearing age. The Population Crisis Committee estimates that in developing countries, 100 to 1,500 deaths occur per 100,000 illegal abortions.

Broadly speaking, abortion laws are liberal in industrialized countries, especially those in which a high percentage of the women work, such as the United States and the Soviet Union. The number of abortions that take place in a particular country depend more on the living conditions, such as housing and the extent of urbanization, than on cultural or religious backgrounds.

A woman's educational level also affects her attitude toward abortion. Generally, the greater the level of education, the greater the willingness to have an abortion. For example, in the United States and the Soviet Union, where women are encouraged to go to college, many of them have abortions in order to finish their education.

In the less developed countries and the countries where the majority religion opposes abortion, the laws are restrictive. Organized religion, however, is not as powerful as it was in centuries past. It certainly does not deter many women from seeking abortions. It means that women get them done illegally, generally under unsafe conditions in the "back alleys." In poor nations, the crude methods, unsanitary conditions, and lack of medical supplies such as antibiotics make illegal abortions very risky. Bungled illegal abortions cause deaths and serious injuries and also put a burden on the hospitals and health clinics.

Of course, abortion laws discriminate against the poor everywhere. Even where abortion is legal, the poor sometimes have illegal abortions unless the fees are paid by national health insurance. Liberal laws are useless to those who cannot afford to pay a high fee for an abortion.

Abortion is the chief method of birth control in countries where contraception is either not available or rarely used. That is particularly true in Catholic countries because the church opposes not only abortion but birth control as well.

⊁ *Canada*

In Canada, abortions are allowed only when a three-member committee of a hospital staff agrees the abortion is necessary to save the woman's life or to protect her health. Unfortunately, many hospitals do not have committees.

There are many reasons why it is difficult to obtain an abortion in Canada. The abortions have to be performed in a hospital, and because of pressure from the right-to-life groups, abortions are being denied or delayed in some hospitals. After India, Canada has the highest number of second-trimester abortions, which are far more risky than those done in the first trimester. Because of the problems at home, many Canadian women travel to the United States to have abortions.

✿ *Europe*

The history of abortion in Great Britain is very similar to that of the United States. Before 1803, abortion was legal before quickening. That year, however, all abortions were made illegal. In 1861, the Offenses Against the Person Act strengthened the anti-abortion law by making the maximum penalty for performing or having an abortion life imprisonment. Although the law affected the woman, it was rarely directed against her. It was aimed at the "back-street surgeons," or abortionists. The law was vague when it came to whether or not it permitted an abortion to save a woman's life. That gray area was often debated and was ultimately tested.

The Offenses Against the Person Act was still in effect in 1939 when a prominent doctor, Alex Bourne, performed an abortion on a fourteen-year-old girl. She had been raped by several soldiers and had become pregnant as a result. Bourne performed the abortion and then called the police. He was arrested and put on trial. In his defense he argued that the abortion was legal because it was done to save her mental health, which was equivalent to saving her life. The judge instructed the jurors to acquit the doctor if they felt he had acted in good faith. He was acquitted, but in spite of this the legal boundaries of abortion remained blurred.

Over and over again, there were attempts in Parliament to pass a new, more liberal abortion law. Finally, a new abortion law was passed in 1967 that applied to England and Wales, but not to Northern Ireland, where abortion is still illegal. Under the new law, abortion was permitted only if two doctors agreed it was necessary for the following reasons: to safeguard the woman's mental or physical health; to ensure that the well being of her other children was not threatened; and to abort a fetus with abnormalities. Abortion was also allowed when carrying the pregnancy to term was a greater risk than the abortion—greater to the woman and her "existing children." This reason was added, ironically, by opponents of the new liberal law, but it had the effect of making an abortion easier to obtain.

Among the factors leading to the change in the abortion law was the high number of illegal abortions and the resulting medical complications and deaths. As in the United States, abortions were more readily available for middle-class or upper-class women. They went to doctors willing to swear that the abortion was needed for psychiatric reasons. Such abortions were technically legal, but were expensive.

As soon as the new law went into effect, the number of legal abortions performed yearly rose from 17,500 to over 35,000. Actually, the increase was a continuation of a trend begun before the new law was passed. Therapeutic abortions had risen from about 1,600 in 1958 to 3,300 in 1964. The new law accelerated this trend.

The sharp increase of abortions put a strain on the medical system, which consists of mostly free national hospitals. A newsletter published by the Abortion Law Reform Association in 1968 stated, "It is no longer the law that is preventing women from obtaining NHS [National Health Service] abortions, it is the attitude of some of the doctors and the shortage of NHS facilities."

The influx of foreign women seeking legal abortions also put a strain on the medical system.

In England, as in the United States, right-to-life groups have been quite active. Although 62 percent of the population in England approves of legal abortion, the Society for Protection of the Unborn Child lobbied to add restrictions to the 1967 Act. Several bills to restrict abortion have been introduced in Parliament and defeated. In 1981, the Department of Health and Social Security issued new guidelines permitting abortions only for medical reasons. These guidelines are not rigidly applied. Nevertheless, they are chipping away at abortion rights in England and Wales.

The laws vary greatly, of course, but most European countries now permit at least some legal abortions. France and Greece allow abortion on request. Abortions are allowed for medical and social reasons in Austria, Bulgaria, West Germany, Hungary, Poland, and elsewhere.

Even in countries where Catholics are in the majority, abortions—both legal and illegal—are common. Many of these countries, such as Italy, have reformed their abortion laws in recent years. But even when abortion was illegal, it flourished.

Italy reformed its abortion law in 1978 to allow any woman eighteen years of age or older to obtain an abortion in the first ninety days of the pregnancy for the following reasons: to protect the physical or mental health of the woman; to end a pregnancy resulting from rape; to abort a fetus with abnormalities; and to end a pregnancy when the woman is financially distressed. In

1981, the voters were asked to decide if they wanted to allow abortions only to protect the woman's health. The proposition was defeated by almost 70 percent of the vote.

Time found in the 1960s that abortion was the chief method of birth control in Spain, where abortion was then illegal. A new abortion law went into effect in August 1986 that permits abortion when the pregnancy is a result of rape, when the fetus is abnormal, or when there is a danger to the woman.

Feminists in Spain do not feel the law is liberal enough, and they have protested against it. During a women's convention held in November 1985, they flouted the law by saying that two abortions had been performed at the convention that did not meet the conditions set by the law.

On the other side of the issue is the National Council of Bishops of the Roman Catholic Church. They oppose all abortions and plan to excommunicate anyone who cooperates in an abortion.

Because of the conflict between the anti-abortionists and the prochoicers, many doctors refuse to perform abortions. Once they are labeled abortionists, their careers suffer and their practices drop.

In Greece, abortion used to be the main method of birth control, although it was illegal. Finally in 1986, the Greek Parliament passed a new law allowing women to have abortions on demand and at state expense. It's estimated that 56 percent of all Greek women have abortions, and that for every birth there are two abortions.

In general, the Scandinavian countries have the most

liberal abortion laws. In 1939, both Denmark and Sweden allowed abortion by official permission for both medical and psychological reasons. There was a sharp increase in legal abortions. The number of illegal abortions also remained high because many women did not want to go through the "red tape." They did not want to fill in the forms and risk refusal. Until 1963, a medical board had to give its permission for abortion in Sweden. In 1963, the law was reformed to allow abortions for fetal abnormalities.

Nevertheless, there were many Swedish women who went to Poland for abortions because they were easier to obtain there. In 1965, a newspaperman who arranged trips to Poland for women seeking abortions was prosecuted, and the uproar over it led the way to more liberal policies.

Today, abortion is allowed on request in Denmark, Norway, and Sweden. Sweden allows abortion on request during the first eighteen weeks of pregnancy.

Abortion is allowed for a wide variety of medical and social reasons in Finland, Iceland, and Luxembourg. In Belgium, abortion is only allowed to save the life of the woman, but it is easy for women to go to the Netherlands or elsewhere where abortions can be obtained.

The Eastern European Communist Bloc

In general, the Communist countries in Eastern Europe and elsewhere have liberal abortion laws for two reasons. First, birth control pills or devices are either scarce or are not used widely. The use of birth control pills has spread very slowly through Eastern Europe.

116 · *The Abortion Controversy*

Second, chronic housing shortages and economic problems make it important for individuals and for the countries to limit the number of births.

Abortion is available on request in the Soviet Union, Austria, and Yugoslavia. In countries such as Poland, Bulgaria, Czechoslavakia, Hungary, and Romania it is allowed for medical and social reasons. In several countries such as Hungary, the abortion laws have fluctuated; sometimes they have been very liberal, at other times restrictive.

The Soviet Union made its abortion laws very liberal in 1955, and the Communist countries in Eastern Europe, except East Germany, followed suit. The Soviet Union has gone back and forth between having liberal and strict abortion laws. Abortion was illegal from 1917 to 1920; from 1920 to 1937 it was legal—and then the law was reversed again. In 1955, abortion on demand was made legal. It was intended as a temporary measure to eliminate illegal abortions and the profit gained from them, and to grant women more freedom. It was also a last resort for unwanted pregnancies, as birth control was not readily available. Birth control still isn't easy to get and it's estimated that on average a Russian woman undergoes six abortions in her lifetime.

Poland, Hungary, and Bulgaria liberalized their abortion laws in 1956. Czechoslovakia liberalized its laws in 1958, Yugoslavia in 1960, and East Germany in 1965. In Czechoslovakia, East Germany, Yugoslavia, and Hungary, a woman needed the approval of a medical commission to get an abortion, but such approvals were easily obtained. In Poland, a woman only had to go to her family doctor.

In 1969, Yugoslavia further liberalized its abortion laws to make abortion available, in effect, on request. Besides allowing abortion for the usual reasons, it allowed abortion "when it can be reasonably expected that the pregnant woman will find herself placed . . . in difficult personal, family, or material conditions, which cannot be remedied by any other means."

Hungary changed its abortion law in 1956 to allow abortions "exclusively on the request of the pregnant woman, not requiring any special social or sanitary indications." Abortion on demand was only allowed in the first twelve weeks of a pregnancy, and the medical boards often attempted to convince women not to have an abortion. Nevertheless, the abortion rate in Hungary was the highest of all the Eastern European countries. It was common for women to have repeat abortions. In 1964, 22 percent of the women who had an abortion in 1963 had a second abortion.

Until the late 1960s, there was no effective birth control program in Hungary, which contributed to the high number of abortions—an estimated average of three per lifetime for a married woman. Abortion was viewed with disfavor by many officials. It was considered a stop-gap method of controlling the population until birth control was more readily available.

In the late 1960s, Hungary reversed its policy—only women over forty were entitled to abortion on demand. Later it lowered the age limit to thirty-five years of age. Abortions for younger women have to meet the usual conditions, such as the pregnancy endangering the woman's health or the presence of fetal abnormalities. Despite the more restrictive law, Hungary has a very high abortion rate. Estimates say that as many as 60 percent of all pregnancies are intentionally terminated.

Czechoslovakia, Bulgaria, and Romania, like Hungary, liberalized their laws and then restricted them in the 1960s. Romania had once allowed abortions on request. Women went directly to a hospital or clinic; there were no restrictions up to twelve weeks. Birth control was rarely used and the abortion rate was very high. Then in 1966, Romania drastically changed its abortion laws, in part because the government was unhappy about the very low birthrate. Only women over forty years of age were allowed abortions on request. Younger women were allowed abortions only if the pregnancy was the result of a rape; there was a risk to her life; there was a possibility that the woman would give birth to a deformed child; or if the woman was in danger of physical, psychological, or emotional trauma. Actually, the new law was liberal in comparison to American laws in force at the time. To increase the number of births, Romania gave cash bonuses to new mothers. Nevertheless, it's now estimated that 60 percent of all Romanian pregnancies end in abortion, and Romania has one of the lowest birthrates in Europe.

Bulgaria ended abortion on request in 1967, except for women over forty-five years of age and for women with three or more children. Women without children are denied abortions except for serious medical reasons, and women with one or two children are dissuaded but not forbidden to have an abortion.

East Germany went a different route. After World War II it passed liberal abortion laws but it tightened its laws in the 1950s and did not relax them again until

1965. The new regulations applied primarily to women under sixteen or over forty, to women with five or more children, and to women whose children were born in rapid succession.

Abortion laws in the Eastern bloc countries are often tied to the governments' efforts to increase or decrease the birthrates, depending on the needs of the times.

The Middle East

During the British Mandate of Palestine in 1936, abortion was banned except to save the woman's life. This ruling was in conjunction with British law, so in 1938 when the British allowed abortions if the pregnancy endangered the woman physically or mentally, Palestine followed suit.

When Israel was founded in 1948, the abortion law was not changed, but in 1952, an Israeli court ruled that abortion was permissible more generally if performed in good faith by a doctor under proper medical conditions. Now, because of the threat of the Arab nations surrounding Israel and the frequent border clashes, the government is attempting to encourage women to have more children.

Some Middle Eastern countries, such as Iran and Iraq, have restrictive laws, but abortion is not unusual, and it is easy to obtain in Iran for upper-class women who can afford the high fees.

Japan

Throughout Japanese history, both abortion and female infanticide were common until the end of the 1800s. Abortion became very common again after

World War II. Japan made abortions easy to obtain to control the growth of the population and to restore the economy, which was in a state of ruin. By 1952, abortions were done at the discretion of the doctors authorized to perform them. This amounted to abortion on demand. A woman had only to say that she needed an abortion for one of the reasons approved and the doctor was not required to check up on her.

By 1953, there were over one million legal abortions performed per year. The figure remained steady until the 1960s, when it dipped to 747,000 and then climbed back up to over 1,500,000 in 1972.

It is likely that Japanese women have abortions primarily because of social or economic conditions. A large number of them, however, say it is for health reasons. The major religions of Japan—Buddhism, Confucianism, and Shintoism—do not strongly oppose abortion. The followers of Shinto do not believe the fetus is a person; the Buddhist leaders accept abortion when the woman has what they consider to be good reasons for having one; and Confucian tradition is ambiguous about abortion.

Yet there are modern Japanese women who are uncertain about the morality of abortion, possibly because it conflicts with the concept of *taikyo*. Taikyo is the belief that the fetus can be "taught" while in the womb. Such a concept obviously implies that the fetus is a person, so many women do feel guilty about having an abortion. Despite their mixed emotions and feelings of guilt, the number of abortions has been high in proportion to live births from the 1950s to the present.

Contraception was relatively ineffective for a long time because until recently neither birth control pills nor IUDs were sold in Japan. The medical profession worried about the side effects of each.

Prime Minister Eisaku Sato, speaking to the Japanese Parliament in 1967, said,

> In the past ten years or so, some civil leaders, social critics, religious authorities, government officials, and political members in Japan have been concerned about the widespread resort to induced abortion. They have been worried over the general tendency to ask for it so easily and so readily. Campaigns to appeal to the general masses not to seek an abortion have been organized on the ground of its moral unwholesomeness and possible health hazards.

From 1968 to 1970, the abortion rate dropped, but it soon went back up to over one million per year.

India

Despite its enormous overpopulation, India had very restrictive abortion laws until recently. The penalty for inducing an early abortion was up to three years in prison and/or a fine, and if the woman was "quick with child," the penalty was up to seven years and/or a fine. Now abortion is allowed for medical and social reasons.

The government has put its efforts into developing family-planning programs, including distributing information about birth control and providing incentives for sterilization.

Given the overcrowding and the extreme poverty in India, estimates that up to 3.9 million illegal abortions took place per year in the late 1960s are easy to accept. The widespread practice of abortion, particularly in rural areas, violates the law and the tenets of Hinduism, the religion of the majority.

China

Because it is faced with great overpopulation, China not only allows abortion, but encourages it informally. Officially, the government tells women to use birth control, yet there are widespread reports that women are pressured into having abortions if they get pregnant after having had their first child. Community leaders "talk" to them about the benefits of having only one child.

In 1981, an incentive program to control the number of births was established. Couples who pledged not to have more than one child were given more money for their work, better housing, and larger pensions. They were also promised a better education for their child. About 57 percent of Chinese couples promised not to have a second child. Those who did had to repay the benefits.

For over twenty years, the government has made extensive efforts to promote family planning. It encourages women to use contraceptives and promotes sterilization. Ironically, as the use of contraceptives has gone up, the number of abortions has also increased, presumably because of increased sexual intercourse. Even the "barefoot" doctors—those who travel around the rural countryside—perform abortions using portable suction equipment.

Africa

In general, the countries of Africa have restrictive abortion laws, but illegal abortions are frequently performed or self-induced. Naturally, the number of injuries and deaths from the complications of illegal abortions is very high, particularly among the poor, because of the unsanitary conditions and lack of medical supplies.

There are exceptions. Ghana, Zimbabwe, and Liberia allow abortions when the pregnancy is a threat to the woman's life or health and in cases of rape or genetic abnormalities. Zambia has the most liberal law in Africa—it allows abortions for social or economic reasons.

Latin America

The abortion laws of the Latin American countries are the most restrictive in the world. This is a reflection of the dominance of the Catholic Church. Yet there is a wide difference between what church officials preach and what women do. Illegal abortions are everyday occurrences. Because most of them are self-induced by using a rod or probe, the number of complications is very high.

Anywhere from 25 percent to 50 percent of all pregnancies end in induced abortions. In Brazil, about 50 percent of all pregnancies end in abortion, despite the laws forbidding abortion except to save the life of the woman or to end a pregnancy resulting from rape. Many women travel to Brazil to obtain abortions there.

In Argentina and Uruguay, abortions are not too difficult to obtain from doctors, even though they are illegal except in rare instances. In the past, abortion was banned in both Mexico and Puerto Rico, yet both places were thriving centers for illegal abortions, performed by midwives or self-induced. Middle- and upper-class women from the United States and Canada were easily able to get abortions.

In Mexico, birth control pills are available without a prescription, yet studies show that a high percentage of the women do not know about birth control. Abortion is legally restricted but extremely commonplace, and deaths from induced abortions are the leading cause of death among women. Yet prosecutions for illegal abortion are rare. Puerto Rico allows abortion on request during the first trimester.

For many women in South America, the only alternative to a self-induced abortion is having the child, but later they may deny him or her medical treatment when ill. This kind of "masked" infanticide takes place commonly in countries like Peru and Colombia. In Peru, women who have abortions are sometimes jailed for up to three years. Women there are in a double bind: birth control is labeled a "sin" but sex is considered a wife's duty.

ELEVEN

Conclusion

The controversy over abortion is not likely to end soon. In fact, it is probable that the debate will become even more bitter in years to come because medical advances will generate further moral and ethical problems. For example, it's possible that viability, or the time when the fetus can live outside the womb, will be established earlier in pregnancies.

When abortion was legalized in 1973, the Supreme Court gave the states the right to ban abortions after viability, which it stated was generally at twenty-eight weeks, but possible at twenty-four weeks. At that time, many twenty-eight-week-developed babies died. Today, nearly all of them survive; many twenty-six-week-developed babies live, and those less developed have occasionally survived for short periods.

It's commonly stated that since 1973 viability occurs

earlier in pregnancy because premature infants that would have died then would live today. But in the opinion of most experts, viability has not been pushed back to earlier than the Court's lower limit. Many experts are very skeptical about reports that a fetus less developed than at twenty-four weeks survives at all, because a doctor can easily miscalculate the gestation period by as much as four weeks.

Dr. Michael Burnhill, obstetrician and gynecologist at the College of Medicine and Dentistry of New Jersey, feels that a twenty-four-week fetus can only be kept alive for a short time—hours or days—because its lungs are not developed. Its blood vessels are so small that it is all but impossible to insert tubes in them to feed it. Its chances of long-term survival are close to zero.

Nevertheless, it is possible that modern technology will, at some point in the future, cause viability to occur earlier. If that happens, will a woman's right to an abortion be threatened? What will happen if viability is pushed back to the first trimester? It is already possible to treat a fetus inside the womb. For example, a fetus can be given a blood transfusion. Will the concept of the unborn versus the born become obsolete?

In the meantime, advances in fetal care are already presenting doctors with ethical problems. Fetuses that were intended to be aborted have, on rare occasions, been born alive, making several doctors' nightmares come true. According to the New York State and City Health Departments, out of 160,000 abortions performed in 1982, there were 18 live births.

An abortion that ends in a live birth presents doctors with an almost overwhelming moral problem. Should doctors attempt to save the fetus just as they would attempt to save a premature infant? A doctor in Philadelphia has been charged with murder because he did not try to save a fetus that lived for ninety minutes after an abortion.

To protect themselves and their staffs, some hospitals established a policy that makes it mandatory to save the fetus. But should the doctors attempt "heroic" measures to save it, or allow nature to take its course?

To avoid the risk of having a fetus survive an abortion, doctors have begun to use methods sure to kill it. In many hospitals, they have established a cut-off date for abortions at twenty weeks. Many doctors have established lower personal limits to protect themselves from a legal suit.

Further advances in fetology are now on the horizon and raising questions among medical experts. At the University of California, experiments have been done in which the embryo has been taken out of one woman and put into another. If that becomes a standard medical procedure, it will raise more questions about abortion. If a surrogate mother—a woman willing to bear the child—offers to give birth to the fetus, would the natural mother still be allowed to abort? Or, could she no longer argue in those circumstances that she has a right to control of her body? Would a woman's right to an abortion still be considered a "personal" right? Or, if a woman did not want to carry a pregnancy to term, would the father be allowed to insist that the embryo be implanted in a surrogate mother?

Researchers are currently working to create an artificial womb. This invention is still a long way off because of the technical difficulties and the staggering costs. But if and when that day does come, will an aborted fetus born alive be placed in an artificial womb, or will that fall into the category of "extraordinary means to save a life"? In the past, the courts have ruled that it is not necessary for doctors to use "extraordinary" means to save a life, for example, when the patient is brain dead. If the day comes when an embryo only days old can be placed in an artificial womb, will the father have the right to insist that it be done even though the mother wants to abort?

These are among the many questions that modern technology is possibly going to pose in the future. That future may be relatively close or quite distant. In the meantime, it's likely that abortion policies will continue to arouse emotional disagreements.

Selected Bibliography

"Abortion Terrorism: The Toll Rises," *Ms.* (March 1985), p. 19.

Balamaci, Marilyn, and others. "Choice vs. Life," *People* (August 5, 1985), p. 69.

Barr, Samuel J., with Dan Abelow. *A Woman's Choice.* New York: Rawson, 1977.

Bouchier, David. *The Feminist Challenge.* New York: Schocken, 1984.

Brody, Baruch. *Abortion and the Sanctity of Human Life: A Philosophical View.* Cambridge, Mass.: MIT Press, 1975.

Callahan, Daniel. *Abortion: Law, Choice and Morality.* New York: Macmillan, 1970.

Clendinen, Dudley. "Abortion Clinics Are Targets Again," *New York Times* (December 9, 1985), p. II, 9.

Clendinen, Dudley. "The Abortion Conflict: What It Does to One Doctor," *New York Times Magazine* (August 11, 1985), p. VI, 18.

Deckard, Barbara. *The Women's Movement.* New York: Harper & Row, 1975.

Degler, Carl N. *At Odds: Women and the Family in America from the Revolution to the Present.* New York: Oxford University Press, 1980.

Dolan, Edward F., Jr. *Matters of Life and Death.* New York: Franklin Watts, 1982.

Dornblaser, Carole, and Uta Landy. *The Abortion Guide: A Handbook for Women and Men.* New York: Playboy Paperbacks, 1982.

Edmunds, Lavinia. "'Silent Scream' Reverberations," *Ms.* (June 1985), p. 89.

Emmens, Carol A., "The Outcry over 'The Silent Scream,'" *Sightlines* (Summer/Fall 1985), p. 14.

Fischkin, Barbara. "D.A. Pickets Abortion Clinic," *Ms.* (December 1985), p. 19.

Francis, Roberta. League of Women Voters of New Jersey. *Public Policy on Abortion.* Trenton, N.J. 1982. Pamphlet.

Francke, Linda Bird. *The Ambivalence of Abortion.* New York: Random House, 1978.

Ganz, Richard L., ed. *Thou Shalt Not Kill.* New York: Arlington House, 1978.

Gordon, Linda. *Woman's Body, Woman's Right.* New York: Grossman, 1976.

Hymowitz, Carol, and Michaele Weissman. *A History of Women in America.* New York: Bantam Books, 1978.

Isaacson, Walter. "The Battle Over Abortion," *Time* (April 6, 1981), p. 20-24.

Jaffe, Frederick S., and others. *Abortion Politics.* New York: McGraw-Hill, 1981.

Klemesrud, Judy. "NOW Plans Drive to Uphold Abortion Right," *New York Times* (July 21, 1985), p. I, 20.

Korones, Susan, and Barbara Costikyan. "Abortion: Your Right under Attack," *Cosmopolitan* (October 1985), p. 222.

Koukoutchos, Brian. "A No-Win Proposal on Abortion Rights," *New York Times* (July 25, 1985), p. I, 23.

Kuker, Kristin. *Abortion and the Politics of Motherhood.* Berkeley: University of California Press, 1984.

Maguire, Daniel C. "A Catholic Theologian at an Abortion Clinic," *Ms.* (December 1984), p. 129-32.

Morgan, Robin, ed. *Sisterhood Is Powerful.* New York: Random House, 1970.

New Jersey Religious Coalition for Abortion Rights. *The Issue Is Freedom! Not Abortion.* Pamphlet.

Noonan, John T., ed. *The Morality of Abortion: Legal and Historical Perspectives.* Cambridge, Mass.: Harvard University Press, 1970.

Pilpel, Harriet F., and others. *Abortion: Public Issue, Private Decision.* Public Affairs Committee, 1975. Pamphlet.

Pollitt, Katha. "Hers," *New York Times* (January 2, 1986), p. III, 2.

Press, Aric, with Ann McDaniel. "A Court in Collision," *Newsweek* (January 14, 1985), p. 20-29.

Quindlen, Anna. "Hers," *New York Times* (March 13, 1986), p. III, 2.

Religious Coalition for Abortion Rights. *25 Protestant, Jewish, Catholic, and other Religious Organizations Committed to Safeguarding the Option of Legal Abortion Rights.* Washington, D.C. 1978. Pamphlet.

Rothman, Sheila M. *Woman's Proper Place.* New York: Basic Books, 1978.

Sass, Lauren R. *Abortion: Freedom of Choice and Right to Life.* New York: Facts on File, 1978.

Schiffer, Robert L. "Hostages to U.S. Abortion Politics," *New York Times* (November 11, 1985), p. I, 19.

Schumacher, Edward. "Spain Law Allowing Some Abortions Takes Effect," *New York Times* (August 4, 1985), p. I, 9.

Seligmann, Jean, and others. "America's Abortion Dilemma," *Newsweek* (January 14, 1985), p. 20.

Sharpe, Rochelle. "Abortion: America's Holy War," Bridgewater, N.J. *Courier-News* (January 20, 1986), p. 1.

Sharpe, Rochelle. "Rev. Stone and His Ghoulish Tactics," *Ms.* (August 1985), p. 20.

"The Silent Scream," *Newsweek* (February 25, 1985), p. 37.

Spake, Amanda. "The Propaganda War over Abortion," *Ms.* (July 1985), p. 92.

Taylor, Stuart, Jr. "Justices Uphold Abortion Rights by Narrow Vote," *New York Times* (June 12, 1986), p. I, 1.

Tifft, Susan. "Explosions over Abortion," *Time* (January 14, 1985), p. 16.

Toner, Robin. "Abortion Battle Shifts to Aid for Family Planning," *New York Times* (February 5, 1986), p. I, 24.

Toth, Ronald S. "The Plain Truth about Abortion! Why So Little Understood?" *The Plain Truth* (May 1985), p. 2.

"U.S. Churches Debate Abortion, South Africa, and Pornography," *Christianity Today* (September 6, 1985), p. 64-65.

Wagenvoord, James, and Peyton Bailey. *Men: A Book for Women.* New York: Avon, 1978.

Who Shall Live? Man's Control over Birth and Death: A Report Prepared for the American Friends Service Committee. New York: Hill & Wang, 1970.

Woodward, Kenneth L., with Mark D. Uehling. "The Hardest Question," *Newsweek* (January 14, 1985), p. 29.

Zintl, R. T. "New Heat over Old Issue," *Time* (February 4, 1985), p. 17.

Index

Abortion
    demographics, 12–14
    funds, 66–74
    history of, 96–107
    illegal, 30–32, 51, 53,
        71–72, 94–95, 109
    and the individual,
        7–23
    induced, 7
    methods, 8–12
    opponents, 32–36,
        84–93
    psychological effects,
        18–21
    reasons for, 14–18,
        27–29
    risks, 11, 30–32, 53,
        107

    role of male, family and
        friends, 21–23
    saline, 9–10
    spontaneous, 7
    suction, 9
    supporters, 24–32,
        93–95
Adoption, 29
Africa, 123
Akron (Ohio), 78–79, 80,
    81
American Law Institute,
    47–48, 55
American Medical
    Association (AMA),
    103–104
Amniocentesis, 15–16, 17,
    20

Arizona, 82
Armstrong, A. James, 61

Barr, Samuel, 23
Bayh, Birch, 61, 62
Bellotti v. *Baird,* 78
Birth control, 12–13, 54,
    106, 121
    condoms, 13, 54
    diaphragms, 12, 13, 54
    "homemade" devices,
        13
    IUDs, 12, 13, 54, 59,
        80
    pills, 11, 12, 54
Birth defects, 15–16, 20,
    27, 28
Blackmun, Justice, 42, 81
Blacks, 12
Bours, Peter, 87–88
Brain, 4
Brennan, Justice, 70
Buckley, James, 58, 64
Burger, Warren, 80–81, 82

Califano, Joseph, 64
California, 41, 54–55, 56
Callahan, Daniel, 36
Canada, 110
Carter, Jimmy, 63, 64, 69
Catholic Church, 26–27,
    36–39, 52, 61, 98–100,
    113–114
China, 96, 122

Chlorionic villus biopsy, 15
Church, Frank, 62
Clay, William, 72
Collauti v. *Franklin,* 76
Colorado, 54, 56, 73
Comstock Act, 105
Connecticut, 102
Constitution (U.S.), 1–2,
    33, 37, 42–43, 45,
    58–62, 66, 69–70
Contraception. *See* Birth
    control
Coop, C. Everett, 17

Danforth v. *Planned
    Parenthood of Central
    Missouri,* 77–78
Death, 4–5, 11, 30, 31,
    110, 124
De Beauvoir, Simone, 32
Dilation and curettage, 9,
    27
Dilation and evacuation, 9,
    10
Discrimination, 51, 68
DNA, 3
Doe v. *Bolton,* 1, 39–44, 57,
    75
Dooling, John, 69

Eagleton, Thomas, 65
Embryo, 3
Europe, 111–119
Euthanasia, 35

Falwell, Jerry, 90
Ferraro, Geraldine, 37
Fetus, 2–5, 92, 125–128
Finkbine, Sherri, 50
Flood, Daniel, 68
Ford, Betty, 63
Ford, Gerald, 63
Francke, Linda, 21
Friedan, Betty, 53

Genetic disorders. *See* Birth
    defects; specific disorders
Georgia, 41–42, 43, 55, 56,
    105
German measles (rubella),
    16, 50–51
Gerster, Carolyn, 35
Goldsmith, Judy, 91, 93, 94
Great Britain, 111–113

Hall, Robert, 49
Harris v. *McRae,* 70
Hatch, Orrin, 65
Helms, Jesse, 65, 66
Hemophilia, 17
Hill, Susan, 84, 90
H.L. v. *Matheson,* 78
Human Life Amendment
    (HLA), 58–62, 64
Human life bills, 66–67
Human Life Federalism
    Amendment (HLFA),
    65–66
Hungary, 117–118

Huntington's chorea, 18
Hyde, Henry, 67, 68
Hyde Amendment, 67–72

Idaho, 83
Illinois, 80
India, 121–122
Informed consent, 78–79
Italy, 113

Japan, 119–121
Jimenez, Rosie, 71–72
Johnson, Douglas, 81

Kennedy, Flo, 30

Latin America, 123–124
Laws, 47–48, 75–76
    lack of enforcement,
        48–51
    liberalization, 54–57
    religious/ethical
        conflicts, 52
    worldwide, 108–124
    See also Supreme Court
Lejeune, Jerome, 33
Lindheim, Barbara, 36
Luker, Kristin, 30, 33

Maguire, Daniel C., 24, 38
Maher v. *Roe,* 70
Maryland, 56
Massachusetts, 55, 72, 78,
    84, 101, 103

McRae v. *Matthews,* 69
Medicaid, 67–73
Menstrual regulation, 8
Methodist Church, 26
Middle East, 119
Miscarriage. *See* Abortion,
  spontaneous
Missouri, 55, 77–78
Mormon Church, 26

Nathanson, Bernard, 92
National Organization for
  Women (NOW), 25, 53,
  90, 93–95
New York, 56, 102–103

O'Connor, Sandra Day, 79,
  82

Packwood, Bob, 66
Pennsylvania, 80, 81
Percy, Walker, 35
Postpartum depression, 21
Pregnancy, 11
Prostaglandins, 10
Protestant Church, 38
Public opinion, 91–93

Quindlen, Anna, 6

Rape, 27, 28
Reagan, Ronald, 33, 56, 67,
  72, 73, 82, 90, 93

Rehnquist, William, 43, 79,
  82
Religion, 19–20, 25–26,
  36–39, 52, 70, 97–100
  See also specific
  religions
Roe v. *Wade,* 1, 39–45, 57,
  58, 61, 65, 67, 75, 76,
  79–83, 104
Roman Catholic Church.
  See Catholic Church
Rosen, Harold, 51
Rossi, Alice, 28
Rudd, Eldon, 68

Scalia, Antonin, 82
Scheidler, Joseph, 86, 89
Schiffer, Robert, 73
Schlafly, Phyllis, 34, 95
Shack, Barbara, 30
"The Silent Scream,"
  92–93
Soviet Union, 108, 109,
  116
Spain, 113
States' rights amendments,
  62–65
Stavis, Richard, 45
Steinem, Gloria, 71, 94
Stewart, Potter, 70
Supreme Court, 1, 39–47,
  57, 58, 63, 67, 70,
  75–83, 104, 125

Teenagers, 12–14

Texas, 40, 41, 42

Thalidomide, 50

Thomas, Lewis, 2

Thomson, Judith, 29

United Nations, 73

Violence, 88–91

White, Byron, 43, 44, 76, 79, 81

Women's rights, 52–54

Zygote, 2–3

About the Author

Carol A. Emmens, formerly a research librarian, is the author of several books for teenagers. They include *John Lennon, The Right to Vote, A Picture Album of Television,* and *A Picture Album of the Sixties.* She also wrote a high interest/ low vocabulary book, *Stunt People and Stunt Work,* which was chosen by *Booklist* as one of the year's best. She is currently the video consultant for the magazine *School Library Journal.* She is the compiler of *Short Stories on Film and Video* and the editor of *Children's Media Marketplace.*

Ms. Emmens has written many articles on a wide variety of subjects: computers, flying, women's rights, cable television, the origins of everyday objects, unique inventions, movies, and television. She has also interviewed many celebrities, among them Jim Henson.

She lives in New Jersey with her teenage son Scott.